BUILDING
IN
EXCELLENCE

**A CHRISTIAN ENTREPRENEUR'S ROADMAP
TO ELIMINATING CONFUSION AND MASTERING
INTEGRITY WHILST BRAND BUILDING**

MARTHINA AMARACHI

To my Parents, thank you for your love, your prayers, and continual support in pursuing my dreams. I love you, always.

To Jennifer, Henry and Florence, thank you for being my pillars of strength and joy, you saw the pretty, the ugly and everything in between.

To my friends, thank you for holding me, being patient with me, supporting me. Thank you for loving me in the same way Jesus would.

To the first cohort of Building in Excellence, thank you for helping bring my vision to life. You will always have a special place in my heart.

To everyone who has being involved up close or from far away; thank you for believing in me.

And finally, but certainly not least, to my best friend, my Lord and my God. Thank You for everything.

To God be the Glory, now and forever. Amen.

Contents

Introduction

Everyone is trying to make a name for themselves, in some capacity at least, whether through a business or their social media presence. It's fair to say that most of us are doing what we can to ensure we leave a strong and positive legacy behind and for a lot of us, our legacy lies in the dreams that we have and our ability to make them a reality.

Through globalisation and the rise of internet access, it has become easy to have access to the tools, resources, and people that can help us materialise our dreams. Think about it; how did you find out about this book? Chances are it was through a platform that required access to the internet, e.g., social media or your email inbox, and not through a flyer at your nearest bus stop or on a shelf in your local library.

It's a great thing to dream big, and an even greater matter to make it a reality. But the truth is, it isn't a quick and easy process. How convenient would it be if, at the snap of our fingers, we could just materialise all our ideas without having to go through weeks, months, and even years of toil? Thankfully, that's not how things work (though with the rise of artificial intelligence, it looks like that's what society is striving for); a great deal of time and effort goes into this process, more than we often anticipate. It goes beyond the marketing strategy and the brand packaging and extends through to your self-awareness; realising your identity and the implication that it has on the way you live your life.

We journey through life, moment by moment and there's no faster route to get to the future (unless you travel to a different time zone if that counts). The same principle applies to the actualisation of your dreams; building in excellence takes time, and you have to go through it step by step to get the most out of it.

This book contains a collection of lessons that I hope will positively shape your journey of building in excellence. Whether it's a brand or a business, your career, or even simply just a relationship with a friend or family member that you're trying to build, each lesson in this book will help you to build solid foundations, that will ensure that all that you do can stand the test of time, outlive you and leave a lasting positive print on the world.

Building in Excellence wasn't written to be read in one go or passively. At the end of each chapter, there will be 2-3 questions for you to ponder on. These questions are designed to provoke action. There will be a space between each question so that you can jot down your initial thoughts, but it doesn't end there. Take at least 20 minutes every time you complete a chapter to reflect on what you've read and make action points that you can put into action as soon as possible. By the time you finish reading this book, it should have highlights, post it notes, pen and pencil scribbles all over from your note taking and usage; you should feel challenged yet encouraged to go the extra mile to live a lifestyle of excellence just like Jesus because excellence is your bare minimum.

This is your personal manual on how to build in excellence.

CHAPTER ONE

Miracles Whilst Building

This book is a miracle in and of itself but in the process of developing this book from an idea to a book in your hands, I've seen so many miracles that have served as testaments of God's faithfulness, His sovereignty, and so much more. Even beyond this book, right through to anything that I've done in life, God has taught me that if I choose to partner with Him, I will see His handprint in my life. I'm to cherish those handprints so that when the storms come, I have a stack of testimonies to hold on to but also, that these moments will be used to encourage others who are coming after, or even at the same stage as me.

Here is one of my stories of God's miracles whilst building.

I was in the process of finally kickstarting my career as a life coach and was deciding on what name to assign to my coaching brand (it's currently under my personal brand). I was torn between three names, all with amazing meanings and in their own way, accurately describing my mission. I could have chosen all three and found a way to fuse them, but I knew I had to only choose one and I wanted God to make it clear to me what name to choose; I wanted confirmation.

Time went by and still, nothing; I hadn't received the strikingly obvious confirmation that I was hoping for. I knew God could and would confirm to me what name to choose especially, because I had involved

Him in the whole process up until this point. I truly wanted my coaching and by extension, my brand to be an expression of Him on the earth. So, I was left with two choices; either wait until He spoke or just pick one and hope that it was the right one. So, I decided to wait.

I was struggling with intense grief at the time. I decided to spontaneously book a daytrip to Toulouse, South France (I'm not spontaneous in nature so this was a one-off and the tickets were only £16. What a deal!). I mainly just wanted a change of scenery but also, it was time for my quarterly get-away; a period dedicated to just being still and knowing that He is God,[1] but to also hear what God was saying concerning the next season.

As my departure date drew closer and I began to plan what I was actually going to do with my time in France, I noticed that I began to develop a preference for one of the names — Auxanō. I made note of this but I didn't officially settle on it. I still wanted it to be undoubtedly obvious. I wanted to know that there was no other valid explanation for this confirmation other than God Himself (I've now grown to realise that this won't always be the case but this time round, God had mercy and extended grace towards me).

Despite all that was going on around me at the time, I had reason to be down in the dumps but to my surprise, I was very excited to discover what

God was going to say to me regarding what was coming next in my life but also to see how God would resolve this brand-name situation.

It was finally the 28th of July. It was around 2a.m. and though I was tired since I hardly got any sleep the night before. I was buzzing; I felt like a little child about to go to Disneyland for the first time (I'm an adult now and I still haven't been to Disneyland, but I assume this is what it'd feel like). I made sure to pack the essentials; I packed my pencil case and my journal because I knew I'd be writing a bunch of things down like my thoughts, prayers, revelations etc; I also packed the book I was reading at the time titled, *God Has a Name* by John Mark Comer (which I would rate as 10/10, and highly recommend). And last but definitely not least, I packed snacks, and toiletries such as a hand sanitiser, and travel documents.

Upon my arrival, I discovered that my mobile data was not working, so I had to rely on public Wi-Fi to be able to use anything like Google Maps to get around. Though it was frustrating, I wasn't too surprised. Something like this had happened whilst I was in Italy earlier that year. I was secretly pleased because it meant I wouldn't be disturbed by any e-mails, messages, or phone calls; I'd be able to get the getaway I was hoping for.

I ended up walking around for a few hours, around the nearby parks, and even stumbled upon a church that was open to visitors. It was completely silent and a place of solitude, leaving room for prayer and meditation, exactly what I was looking for. I sat there for a while just in silence, basking in God's presence. I then journaled for a bit, walked around to see the beautiful paintings that were on display around the building, went outside for a walk in the area, bought some food and repeated this process a few times. For some people, this may seem boring or mundane but for me, it was so refreshing. It was also pouring rain outside, but we won't focus on that.

It was a wholesome day that I really enjoyed, yet, by the time I was in the airport waiting for my flight back to the UK, I still hadn't received the clarity I was yearning for regarding my coaching brand name. I wouldn't be honest if I said I wasn't slightly disheartened by this. I just had to keep reminding myself that even if it wasn't in my time away that I got this confirmation, God had heard my prayers and would answer me in the time He deemed best so I just needed to be patient and continue waiting.

When it comes to flight seats, I'm a window girl only. Whatever the situation, I will not be in the middle seat. The aisle seat is tolerable but like I said, window girl only. So, to avoid disappointment and a distressing flight, I tend to choose my seat. However, shockingly for this particular trip to France, I didn't choose my seat. In retrospect, my mind was occupied with other more important things, and I also didn't want to pay to choose my seats. So, I just prayed that the seats that I was allocated were not middle seats and by God's wonderful grace, I got a window seat on my outbound flight and an aisle seat for my inbound flight.

It was now around 10 p.m. and I had finally boarded my flight. I was seated in the middle of the plane so there were numerous people walking past me, looking for their seats. My row was empty, and I was quietly praying that no one would sit next to me so that I could just move to the window seat after take-off and sleep for the rest of the flight. Once majority of the passengers had boarded the flight and my row was still empty, I was confident that no one else would come to join me. As I began to make myself comfortable, a lady came and asked if she could get by as she had the middle seat. My heart sank. I was now banking on the hope that no one would sit on the last available seat on our row so that I could move across and still have a shot at enjoying the flight. Boarding was now complete, so I asked the lady if I could sit on the window seat after take-off and she said it was fine with her; there was still hope after all.

Somehow after take-off, this lady and I began engaging in conversation. To be honest, I was hoping that it wouldn't last long because I actually wanted to sleep, and I still hadn't switched seats so there was nowhere to rest my head. We ended up speaking for the entire flight, and I'm so happy we did. I found out that she travelled for a living and whilst we were on the flight, she booked a one-way ticket to some place in South America (I can't remember where exactly). She was an art teacher for young kids and that was how she raised the funds to support herself. She had gone through a painful breakup and we spoke a bit about that, too. I told her that I had spent the last couple of months travelling, and that I was a life and relationship coach too, amongst many other things. The meat of our conversation was on the topic of faith; she believed that there was a God but didn't know who He or it was. We also spoke about astrology, and I also shared my beliefs about the Trinitarian God of the Bible.

I took a lot away from our conversation and she said she had a lot of food for thought, too. She even mentioned that what I had shared helped her understand even more on who God is (Glory to God!). This was a conversation I knew I wouldn't forget.

Yet, about 40 minutes into the flight, one of us pointed out that we hadn't exchanged names so I introduced myself as I normally do. "My name is Marthina but it's spelt with a H after the T."

We both laughed and then she introduced herself. "I'm Aux-sana".

I couldn't even reply, I was gobsmacked, and even confused; my whole body just froze for a few seconds but it felt like minutes. Once I caught my breath again, I explained to her that I was in the process of choosing a name for my coaching brand and that I was waiting on God to make it clear to me which name to choose. I went on further to explain that Auxanō was one of the options and that, though I had developed a preference to it, I still wanted a clear confirmation and that she was literally an answered prayer. She too was in shock and also believed that this was the clarity that I had been seeking. She even went on to encourage me and speak words of life over what I was building. I asked her if she knew what her name meant and she said that she wasn't sure but, in some languages, it meant a gift from God (when I searched it up, it meant praise God). My heart was so full, as there was so much to process; I was in awe.

What makes this story juicier is that Auxana, just like myself, didn't pay to choose her seat so she sitting next to me was a 'random' allocation. She continued on to say that she wasn't supposed to be on the flight we were on. She was due to leave France a few days earlier, but due to some unexpected events, she missed her original flight so she was placed on this flight instead as it was the last flight leaving Toulouse that day. The odds of us meeting, and sitting together at the point of our lives was so slim, dare I say impossible, yet God in His beauty and wisdom made it possible.

We continued our chatter and before we knew it, we had landed in London, and it was time to get off the plane. That was the last time I saw Auxana; I didn't even see her on the shuttle bus or at passport control. It was as if she was never on the flight. Whenever I share this story with people, I'm often asked if I thought she was an angel and the truthful answer is I don't know. Whether she was or not, she remains a person sent by God, and someone God used for His glory. As I'm writing this, I'm just as moved as I was when it was happening. I'm reliving it all over again. Can you see how faithful God is? He will confirm His word! He hears our prayers and requests, and He answers them. It wasn't until after I actually launched Auxanō that I truly realised what had happened on that flight. It is such a special testimony and one that I always refer to when I'm lacking motivation or I feel like giving up.

There's a level of confidence you walk with when you know that the Lord is truly with you. There's a level of boldness you walk with when you're partnering with the Lord to build something excellent, that will bring Him the glory He is due.

Sometimes, He shows up loud and clear but other times, He can be very subtle, but the truth remains that He always shows up. It may be a small still voice in your heart [1], other times it may be a dream or a vision, perhaps you're singled out in church and you receive a prophetic word or maybe it's simply the scripture of the day that comes from the Bible App. Remember, whatever you are doing, be it writing a book, starting a small business, a blog, a YouTube channel, or a social media page, remain in communion with God.

I recently watched a short sermon on TikTok by Apostle Michael Orokpo and he said something which was simple yet so profound. He said communication breeds connection and it is so true for all relationships. We need to be in constant communication with the Lord to connect with Him and grow to know His voice in the still winds and in the thunderstorms too.

There are miracles everywhere; you are a miracle, your friends and family are miracles, and what you are building is a miracle. Shift your perspective, build your faith and appreciate the miracles that God gives you whilst building.

Put it into action!

1. What miracles whilst building have you experienced recently and are there any miracles that you haven't taken the time to appreciate?

2. How often do you ask God what He wants you to do?

3. Do you recognise the still small voice of God, as well as His loud thunderous voice? List some examples.

CHAPTER TWO

Excellence Defined

As a child of God, excellence is your default mode; it's the bare minimum. We ought to display excellence in the way that we steward our gifts, talents, and money, the way we treat others, the way we live our daily lives, and much more. You may be thinking, sure Marthina, but this is nothing new, and you're right as this isn't a brand-new revelation but it's a truth I think we gloss over too quickly. We need to understand why it's so important that we truly live a lifestyle of excellence and therefore why we should be building in excellence. Let's begin, shall we?

One definition of excellence is 'the fact or state of excelling; superiority; eminence',[1] another definition is, 'extremely good',[2] and another definition is 'very good of its kind; eminently good'.[3] The general theme is that to be excellent is to stand out, and this is no news for us believers. In Jesus's sermon on the mount, He teaches that we are the light of the world, a city set upon a hill that cannot be hidden. He goes on to say that we should let our lights shine before men so that they may see our deeds and moral excellence so that God in heaven may be glorified.[4]

Furthermore, in Paul's letter to Titus, he encourages Titus to teach with sound doctrine and highlights the importance of setting himself apart as a model of a life nobly lived and with dignity, to demonstrate integrity in all that he teaches.[5] Even Apostle Peter's letter to the persecuted church includes an encouragement that they are to hold on to whilst they suffer in the name of Christ. He reminds them that they are a chosen race, a royal priesthood, a consecrated nation, a [special] people for God's possession.[6] Again, this is a reminder of our calling to stand out.

Looking back in the Old Testament, Daniel who was famously known for being thrown in the lion's den for choosing to worship God instead of the King of the land, was distinguished above the governors and satraps because an excellent spirit was in him.[7] Some translations say an extraordinary spirit, but we know that this was the Ruach (Hebrew word for Spirit) of God at work in him. Prior to Jesus' birth, the Holy Spirit didn't dwell among men; He would come and go as and when needed. But God in His loving mercy, sacrificed His only begotten son, that whoever believes in Him would be given the right to be children of God,[8] and have eternal life.[9] So, through the death and resurrection of Jesus Christ, we have been given the Holy Spirit, who works in us by giving us the desire and power to do what pleases Him.[10] Ultimately, we cannot walk in excellence without the help of the Holy Spirit. It is Him who helps us please God but also helps us find favour in the sight of both God and men.

In the book of Proverbs, we are further reminded that those who excel in their work will stand before kings.[11] Many more scriptures reinforce the definition of excellence, meaning to stand out and be set apart. Therefore, we must hold on to that truth and make every effort to live a lifestyle of excellence because we serve the Lord of Lords — the Lord of Excellence Himself.

The first time the word excellent is used in Scripture is in the book of Esther. Xerxes, King of Susa, decided to throw a banquet in his third-year as king. It involved showing off all the riches of his glorious kingdom and the splendour of his excellent majesty.[12]

The Hebrew word translated into excellent is *tiph'arah tiph'ereth* meaning ornament, beauty, honour, or majesty. It comes from the root word 'pa'r paw-ar' meaning to glorify, gleam, or embellish. Excellence beautifies, and it enhances not only the beauty of your character but even your physical beauty. When you continue to explore the Scriptures, you'll find that when someone or something is described as excellent, it means that he/she is abundant, surpassing, or magnificent.

Excellence doesn't just bring glory to God. It beautifies us, too, but do not let that be a distraction. You can walk in worldly excellence, be beautified, and still miss out on the prize. You can claim to do things excellently in the name of Jesus, and at the end of the day, He will still say you missed the boat; *all you did was use me to make yourself important. You don't impress me one bit.*[13]

Don't be that person. Whatever you do, live your life in a way that glorifies and honours God,[14] and in doing so, you will be walking in excellence — the God-designed way.

Hold on to this as we continue to explore what it truly means to build yourself in excellence.

Put it into Action!

1. At this point in your life, what does building in excellence mean to you?

2. What are you trying to build [in excellence] and why?

3. What steps have you taken already to begin building in Excellence?

CHAPTER THREE

The Character of an Excellent Builder

Okay, so let's talk about character formation and what it has to do with anything. The reality is that our character says a lot about us, more than we may like to admit. This means for us as Christians, our character should reflect the God we serve; it should reflect Jesus.

According to our reliable friend Google, 'character is defined as the 'mental and moral qualities distinctive to an individual'. Synonyms of character include personality, disposition, and temperament. Essentially, your character is the sum of the qualities you possess. Your character is made up of a bunch of personal adjectives, and is often linked with your personality. So, your mindset and perspective will be a key component to what influences your behaviour.

The reason this is so important is because, if your character isn't right, no matter how much good you do, you will never hold a good witness and the scope of your influence will never reach its full potential.

In the Gospel of Matthew, Jesus invited Matthew to be one of His disciples. After accepting this, Matthew later invited Jesus and the other disciples to come and dine at his house. Matthew was a tax collector and was despised by the Jewish community so when the Pharisees saw that Jesus and His disciples were dining at Matthew's house, they were perplexed. They even went on to ask Jesus why He and His disciples dined with sinners, lowlifes, and scums.[1]

Jesus was known as someone who would acknowledge and befriend the marginalised and outcasts of society. This act alone said a lot about Jesus' character, because it showed that He prioritised love, and cared for every individual regardless of what they had done or who they were. Jesus demonstrated an unconditional love that had never been seen in such a capacity before, so that people who had never seen Him but had only heard what He had done were drawn to Him.

In John's Gospel, Jesus met a woman at the well in Samaria. He asked her for some water and she, just like the Pharisees in the previous story, was thrown aback by the request, so much so that she asked Jesus why He would ask her of all people for a drink. For context, Jews had no dealings with Samaritans, so a Jewish man even uttering a word to a Samaritan woman was especially rare.[2] Yet despite knowing this, Jesus felt that he had to go through Samaria even though there were alternative routes to get to His destination. [3] Jesus did what He needed to do, and He dismantled unhealthy societal norms that didn't reflect the Godhead. The fruit of this act was that now, many Samaritans from that city believed in Him and trusted Him [as Saviour] because of what the woman said when she testified of Him. They even asked Jesus to stay with them and He did, for two days![4] Can you imagine that? He didn't just speak to a societal outcast, but He even dwelt amongst them. What a wonderful God we serve! His character speaks nothing short of love and though we may not find ourselves in situations quite like this, we ought to train our character to utter the language of love.

More personally, an area of my character that God has had to deal with is my thoughts. I had a victim mentality, so I used to think that I had no say in the things that had happened to me and that the consequences were final. I found it difficult to receive advice because I just felt like no one understood me and if you had not experienced what I had experienced, then you automatically were in no place to give me any form of advice. It took lots of prayer, sitting, and dealing with my past, community help, reading the Word, comfort, and the love of God to change that mindset into a growth one — a victorious one. I didn't realise how much more of a compassionate, and empathetic person I could be, now that I had a renewed mind and a renewed character. This compassion and empathy have played a big role in my coaching career and have been a means through which God can take the glory.

You need to know that God wants you to develop your character. Why? As I mentioned before, everything about you can be used to glorify God, and since your character speaks louder than your words, this is definitely a means through which God can use you.

Character development can be done through God disciplining us and teaching us the right way in which we should go.

Here are a few Scriptures that talk about God's correction:

But don't, dear friend, resent God's discipline.
Don't sulk under His loving correction.
It's the child He loves that God corrects;
a father's delight is behind all this.
Proverbs 3:11-12 [MSG]

Therefore, know in your heart (be fully cognizant) that the Lord your God disciplines and instructs you just as a man disciplines and instructs his son.
Deuteronomy 8:5 [AMP]

He who neglects and ignores instruction and discipline despises himself, But he who learns from rebuke acquires understanding [and grows in wisdom].
Proverbs 15:32 [AMP]

God wants to shape your character because He wants your life to improve not just so that you can become a better person, but so that you can excel in all that you do. Also, in developing your character, you have a better shot at building in excellence.

So, what does this look like you ask?

Often times, your character will be shaped by the experiences you face. 'X is testing my patience', is a phrase that I'm confident you've either heard or you've said yourself. In the first chapter of James, the Lord's

Brother's epistle, he says, 'Consider it a sheer gift, friends, when tests and challenges come at you from all sides. You know that under pressure, your faith-life is forced into the open and shows its true colours. So don't try to get out of anything prematurely. Let it do its work, so you become mature and well-developed, not deficient in any way.'[5] When our faith is tested, the more our faith grows and our character is shaped. It's just like anything else which also takes time, so don't expect to see changes overnight (though by God's grace, this is possible too).

Let's now look at how you can practically ensure that your character is consistently being developed to glorify God.

First of all, ask those around you. Something that I like to do is to ask my friends about myself. I was doing a devotional one day and it had me thinking about what motivates me, compared to what my friends and family think motivates me. So, I messaged a few friends and family and asked them what they thought my driving force was. Many people said my faith, and others added my sense of responsibility and/or my desire to help others in any capacity that I can. When I placed it against what I believed my sense of responsibility was, I was then able to see where things misaligned or aligned and why and from there, I was able to think about what practical steps I could take to communicate the correct message.

Secondly, ask God. This is an obvious one that we may forget to do as often as we should. Try to carve out time regularly, (it could be weekly, bi-weekly, monthly etc.) where you ask God to highlight the areas of your character or personality that are not accurately reflecting Him. He will show you and though at first you may be in denial or even offended by what He revealed to you, it is important that you know that God loves you and, in this love, He will correct you and discipline you so that you walk in the right path for His namesake. The writer of Hebrews reminds us that, 'for a moment, all discipline seems painful rather than pleasant, but later, it yields the peaceful fruit of righteousness to those who have been trained by it'.[6] So despite how you feel, thank Him for disciplining and correcting you. Remember, He won't just reveal it to you and leave you there but He will lead you in the path of righteousness,[7] and lead you to the way of everlasting life.[8] Just trust Him and hang in there.

Last but not least, audit yourself. Sometimes we don't really need God to reveal it to us in a dream or through a prophetic word, nor do we need to conduct a whole research project to find out where we may be thriving or falling short in. Sometimes, we just need to cultivate a habit of self-awareness and in doing so, we'll be able to identify our strengths and weaknesses more often rather than being surprised.

Something that I like doing is to sit down with a blank sheet of paper and just write down what comes to mind when I think about my strengths, skills, and development areas. Though these things may not lay in our conscious mind, they definitely do lie within our subconscious mind and when we tap into that, we give ourselves the space to see beyond the surface level.

The key thing with this activity is to be true to yourself, because no one will see this apart from yourself (and God), unless you choose to share it with someone else. You need to be willing to accept that there are parts of you that aren't actually all that great, because Scripture says, 'for all have fallen short of the glory of God'.[9] The more you look within yourself, the more you'll realise that you probably have an inflated sense of self.

The rise of personal development in society is great. I'm an advocate for self-development to be taught and encouraged in all spheres of life because after all, I'm a life coach. But where I think we as a society have gone wrong is where there is a slight overemphasis on self-actualisation, which according to Maslow's hierarchy of needs, is the point at which an individual reaches full potential and is the highest on the hierarchy.

Personal development often tells you to look within yourself to find strength, and gold. It either tells you to do this and you'll become great or do that and you'll become successful. Though it contains some elements of truth, it is not the full truth. Personal development starts first and foremost in God, so look to Him and He will reveal to you where you need to work on whether blatantly or subtly.

Put it into Action!

1. When was the last time you conducted a self-character check and when is your next one?

2. What element of your character are you going to work on over the next month?

3. Is there anyone within your community who has the character of an excellent builder that you can learn from?

CHAPTER FOUR

Integrity:
A Pillar of Excellence

We've just looked at the character of an excellent builder, but I want us to take one step further. If you didn't know before, let me tell you now that you cannot build in excellence without **integrity.** Someone who builds without it can be likened to the foolish man who built his house on sand and when the winds and storms came, it collapsed and was swept away.[1]

If integrity is a quality trait that we should live by, then it must by default translate into the way we build our brands. It's not a finishing touch or just a token to build consumer trust, but it's a way of life, and how we were designed to live by.

Google has two definitions for integrity. The first being is 'the quality of being honest and having strong moral principles' and the second, 'the state of being whole and undivided'. So essentially, it is what society would generally define as being a good person. If you're a good person, you hold integrity and if you hold integrity, you're a good person, right?

If hate is the opposite of love, bad, the opposite of good and sour, the opposite of sweet then what is the opposite of integrity? Dishonesty, division, deceit, incompleteness, disgrace, and dishonour are all antonyms of integrity. Though not entirely surprising, it definitely got me thinking about the impact integrity can have on us as individuals and the brands we build but also the gravity of the impact that a lack thereof could equally have.

Integrity, an article from the Stanford Encyclopaedia of Philosophy, presents the idea that in society we often find that integrity is often interchangeable with morality, yet at the same time, we make a distinction between an individual who acts integrally but not morally. It appears that in some contexts, integrity is the act of displaying honesty and fairness, other times it's goodness, or morality, and other times it's a state of wholeness and undividedness. With so many varying philosophies surrounding integrity, what it is and how we can live it out, it's of utmost importance that we know how God defines integrity so that we can ultimately live a life of integrity, in accordance with God's standards.

In my earlier YouTube days, I was using a software called video editor to edit my videos on my trusty HP Laptop. Unfortunately, or rather, fortunately, my laptop screen broke, so I needed a new one as soon as possible, and not just for editing videos. I had previously recorded and edited videos on my phone before. That was a level of stress I hope I never return to again but because I had assignments to complete and submit and my university exams were online so I needed my laptop to sit them. By God's grace and favour and through my sweet mother, I got a new laptop within a few days, and it was a brand-new MacBook pro!

Since the software I was previously using was not available on my new laptop, I transitioned to iMovie, and though it was a much simpler software to use with fewer features, it did the job, so I couldn't complain. But I still kept my eye out looking for alternatives. I then trialled Final Cut Pro which was nice but it wasn't doing it for me, so I cancelled my subscription after my free trial. Eventually, I tried to find a way to get my old software on my laptop and I found that they had actually developed a version that was iOS compatible, but it had a big price tag that was beyond what I could afford on my student budget. I prayed about it and felt that I could proceed and was also willing to make the sacrifice, but I waited and pondered on it just to be sure it wasn't just my heart trying to deceive me (because the heart is truly deceitful above all else).[2] After a while, I no longer felt the peace to proceed so I chose to wait and see what other provision God would bring in this area. After all, iMovie was working just fine, but I wanted more.

I waited and waited (a sport that I should be a professional at now haha!) and still heard nothing but I found out that there were people out there who would share their login details for their premium accounts for strangers like me to use. There was no catch, none that I ever knew of anyway, and to me, it seemed like a win-win situation. I just saw it like someone sharing their Netflix password with me so I could enjoy its benefits without paying for it myself. I had no issue with this because I was at some point the friend who shared their Netflix password.

After editing a few videos and releasing one using the new (technically old) editing software, I felt a huge conviction. I didn't feel comfortable carrying on my editing on that software and after digging to find out why, I still felt the same way I did; it all began to make sense. It felt like I was deceiving my viewers, how could I create content and edit on a software that I had obtained through what now began to feel like illegitimate means? To some people, this may seem exaggerated, but the truth is I would not have recommended people to do the same thing because there was a hesitance, and an uncertainty about how I went about putting out content. Now I know that I'm not necessarily breaking any laws, and I'm not a criminal but the conviction in me was too strong and I know God demanded higher and better standards from me.

I believed YouTube was a platform that the Lord desired for me to be present on, and up until that point, He had provided and met my every need. I never needed to go through a side road to get something. For example, if I couldn't afford to buy brand new equipment, He would make a way for me to get it second-hand and in great quality too. In hindsight, I realised it was my impatience that led me to the side road but as a follower of Christ who had spoken on authenticity and integrity before, I was aware that I had a responsibility to act with integrity, to be trustworthy, and practice what I preached. So, by choosing to continue using this software, I was choosing the side roads and ultimately compromising my integrity and authenticity; I wasn't willing to carry on in *dishonesty* or *deceit* so I decided to give it up (wasn't as easy as I thought it'd be) and return to my faithful iMovie, and I haven't turned back since.

The point of this story is that integrity is sometimes practiced between yourself and God. No one would have ever known the software I used to edit my videos and how I got access to the software unless they asked, or I told them. So technically, it never really mattered but the reality is they do, and the Scripture says, 'all that is secret will eventually be brought into the open, and everything that is concealed will be brought to light and made known to all'. [3] Even if I didn't say it then, at some point it would have 'caught up with me' and I'm thankful to God for His mercy, because He convicted me of my sin. Was it really a sin? I hear your concern; the Bible says that it is a sin to know what to do and not do it. [4] Remember, integrity is necessary in secret and in public too.

If you thought that was quite personal, let me share with you what the battle for integrity can look like within your personal relationship with God. Prayer in its simplest form is a conversation with God, and a space where both speaking and listening take place. I think back to the days when I was a leader at a Christian fellowship at University, I would teach the Word of God on a weekly basis and I loved it. I enjoyed studying the Word so to be able to teach it was a beautiful blessing.

Initially, I started off having separate times to study the Word of God for myself and prepare for when my next teaching would be, but as time went by and my responsibilities both in and outside of ministry increased, more things demanded my time, and my capacity was almost at full usage. In an attempt to manage this, I found myself using my personal quiet time with God to prepare for a teaching session. I began to take a 'study to teach' approach instead of a 'study to learn' one. What I should have done is kept to consistently studying the Word of God for myself because, it's through this that I would continually be able to know His voice and understand His will, generally and more personally. The goal was never 'study to teach', but study to become more intimate with my Lord, and in that place of intimacy, I also study to teach. So, just to be clear, studying to teach is not bad, but that cannot and should not be the sole motivator for you to study the Word of God.

How does this link to integrity? I remember when I would get ready to prepare for a teaching, I would say prayers that went along these lines, *'Holy Spirit lead me as I study your Word, and may I grow to know you more as I study your Word. Grant me understanding of your Word and show me what it is you want to say to your people'.* Classic Christian minister prayer, right? It's important because of course, you want the Holy Spirit to lead you in your study; you want to grow in knowledge and understanding and you most definitely want to make sure that the Word you will be delivering is what God wants you to share (and that it's Biblical).

However, though I loved teaching (and still do), I would often feel the pressure to ensure that my teaching was perfect. Even though I never said it out loud using those words, my thought processes and attitude would indicate that perfection by my standards was the goal.

In hindsight, though those prayers were great, they weren't an accurate reflection of what was going on in my heart. If I could go back and say a prayer that accurately reflected my heart during that time it would be, *'Lord, I want to make sure I say the right things. I want to make sure I come across as one who is knowledgeable and wise. Lord, don't let anyone see how hard it is for me to study or even pray but just take the wheel. Help me to be perfect and for others to see me as perfect, too'.*

Do you see where I'm going with this? Stay with me, as it'll all tie up nicely at the end.

When we come to God, we ought to be honest, because He wants us to be honest with Him. The Bible says that, *your Father knows what you need before you ask Him.*[5] You cannot deceive God! If you think that by saying the right words you can manipulate God into believing that you are devoted to Him, but your actions suggest otherwise, then you are deceiving no one but yourself; God knows the hearts of men. He knows what the Holy Spirit is thinking.[6] Confess your sin to Him. He's not there to condemn you[7] but He rather encourages you to come boldly before the throne of grace.[8] Remember that He is a faithful and just God so He will forgive you.[9] So go to Him and do so with a genuine heart. A prayer that I hold on to, to help me stay on track is one that King David prayed whilst he was in the wilderness running away from Saul.

Examine me, O God, and know my mind;
Test me, and discover my thoughts. – Psalm 139:23[GNT]

Point out anything in me that offends you,
and lead me along the path of everlasting life. - Psalm 139:24 [NLT]

When you pray this prayer, you allow God to humble you by showing you the thoughts, beliefs, and perspectives that you have, that are not aligned with His will. He will show you areas in your life where you may be putting on a pretence, especially in regard to your relationship with Him. He wants you to be in deep intimacy with Him, so anything that hinders that, He'll want you to get rid of.

Jesus teaches that, out of the abundance of the heart the mouth speaks.[10] I remember having a conversation about this with my friends where we were discussing how this also translates into what we say in prayer, the jokes we make, what we watch or listen to, and even the people we surround ourselves with. All these things affect our heart and our heart influences what we say. Therefore, we can safely conclude that there is a hidden personal truth somewhere in all that you say and it's just a matter of time before you recognise it. This is why it's so important to guard your heart above all else, because from it flows the issues of life.[11] But remember, your heart is also deceitful above all else,[2] so put your trust in God, who searches the heart and examines your mind.[12] Let down your pride and accept that you have fallen short. Don't deceive yourself and believe that you are without fault somewhere, because there is always room to grow and room to improve. Let Jesus mould you and lead you in the path of everlasting life. Let Him lead you in the path of integrity.

By this point, you should have a good understanding of what integrity is and what integrity can look like in your day-to-day living. Now let's look at why it's actually important.

God has integrity. He has never said He will do something and never do it; He keeps to His Word.[13] In Genesis, we are told that God created us in His image, according to His likeness, He formed us.[14] So we, who are made in the image and likeness of an honourable God, ought to display integrity also. We are supposed to be people who do what they say they will do and finish the good works we have started, so that people will ultimately see them and give glory to our Father in Heaven.[15]

Sometimes, it can be tempting especially if we are people pleasers, or we tend to overcommit under the guise of 'helping' but end up underperforming. Would you deem someone who continually makes a promise to help you out with something but always fails to fulfil like a person who has integrity, let alone demonstrate the character of God?

Probably not. The problem of overcommitting and underperforming is not a new problem. It has existed for thousands of years, and it deals with deeper heart issues and if left 'untreated' it can damage the integrity of an individual. The author of Ecclesiastes tells us that, 'it is better not to promise at all than to make a promise and not keep it'.[16] It is better to say 'no' than to say 'yes' at the expense of your integrity.

But remember, a key part of being a light in this world is to have integrity.

Trust and integrity go hand in hand. We have already explored the definitions of integrity and though there may be varying qualities attached to an individual deemed to have integrity, it is clear that such a person is someone you can trust.

Think about it. When hiring managers are looking for a new employee to hire, they do not choose those who are known (via referencing for example) to lack integrity or are known for not keeping their word. Why? Because they can't be trusted, and the employer cannot be sure that the new recruit will stick to this job or will even be able to perform the tasks that they will be allocated to do.

How about your friends? Do any of your friends lack integrity, and if so, to what extent? What about yourself? Are there any areas of your life where you are lacking integrity and how might this be affecting your relationships? We can all agree that we appreciate honesty in others and admire selflessness and sacrificial love; that's why we have superheroes in

TV shows and movies, and why someone who risks their life for the welfare or protection of someone else, is labelled a 'hero'. It's what we yearn for at the core of our being. Within our relationships, be it romantic, platonic, or strictly professional, we desire a safe space; a place where we can be vulnerable and honest, a place where we can be heard and seen, a space where we know we don't have to put up a front and we know that it's okay to not be okay. In our relationships, we look for affirmation and encouragement. We look for the unconditional love that God shows us whether we believe in Him or not. But sometimes, what happens is that we forget to love others the way we would like to be loved or love ourselves. We are encouraged from Scripture to, love our neighbours as we love ourselves[17] and one way in which we can do this is through displaying and living out integrity. Choosing integrity is not always the easiest decision to make but it's always the best decision because it will always be a decision of love (by now we mean unconditional love by God's definition). When you choose to be a person of integrity, people will naturally gravitate towards you because you are someone who can be trusted. Your integrity will speak volumes for you in rooms where you are not physically present.

Jesus being the fullness of God[18] displayed integrity perfectly. When Jesus went into the wilderness, Satan came and tempted Jesus on three separate occasions. *'Again, the devil took him to a very high mountain and showed him all the kingdoms of the world and their glory. And he said to him, "All these I will give you, if you will fall down and worship me." Then Jesus said to him, "Be gone, Satan! For it is written, "'You shall worship the Lord your God and him only shall you serve.'" Then the devil left him, and behold, angels came and were ministering to him.'* [19] The options were there before Jesus; He could have chosen to submit to the devil and surrender all that He is and stands for or stand firm in the truth, stand firm in integrity, and remain faithful to Himself. Thankfully, Jesus chose the latter (otherwise you and I would have very different lives right now). The Word of God is true, so if you are ever in doubt, hold on to the truths of God and you will be okay.

Daniel was someone whose actions reflected his words and his beliefs. Daniel was taken by the Babylonians in exile, because he was a *youth without blemish, of good appearance and skilful in all wisdom, endowed with knowledge, understanding learning, and competent to stand in the king's palace, and to teach them the literature and language of the Chaldeans.* [20]

During this period, King Nebuchadnezzar allocated portions of choice food to these young men, but because Daniel knew that eating those foods would make him ceremonially unclean, he asked the chief of the eunuchs to give him and his friends just vegetables, so that they would not defile themselves.[21] He remained faithful to the laws of God.

Later on, in chapter 6 of the book of Daniel, we read that Daniel stood out amongst the rest of his peers because God had placed in him the spirit of excellence.[22] Daniel's peers were jealous of him and sought to find a ground for complaints against him but were unable to do so because 'He was faithful, and no error or fault was found in him'.[23] His peers knew that he was faithful to God and decided to use this as an opportunity to get rid of him. So, they convinced the king to create a huge statue of himself that everyone living within the provinces under his reign would bow down and worship and no worship of any other god would be permitted. Failure to adhere to these rules meant you would be cast into the lions' den.

When Daniel found out about this, he went to his house and worshipped God exactly the same way that he used to do. Daniel, at no point, compromised his beliefs and faithfulness to God. Though this meant that he was ostracised and persecuted, God kept him and throughout this time, the rulers of his time always showed him great favour.

When the twelve spies were sent to scout the land, only Caleb and Joshua found it to be a land full of milk and honey.[24] Their integrity lay in truly being able to see and believe the promise, despite the odds and believing that God would bring them to the land that He promised them. In doing so, they encouraged the people of Israel and brought about a renewed sense of hope. The other ten men who came back with a negative report, were eventually killed. So, integrity and faith also go hand in hand, as it can also spare your life.

Integrity justifies you. The first time that the word integrity is used in the Bible is in the Book of Genesis chapter 20, when God appeared to King Abimelech in a dream and rebuked him for taking Sarah as his wife. The king defended his case against God by saying that he didn't do anything wrong, because Abraham had presented Sarah as his sister therefore, he was not 'stealing another man's wife' for himself. He didn't do anything deceitfully but was honest in this situation. God affirmed this by saying to Abimelech that He was aware that his actions were done in the 'integrity of his heart' and that it was God Himself who kept him from sleeping with her.

Remember, God knows what goes on in your heart and despite the heart being deceitful, it is important that we continue to strive to do all things with integrity because when we are questioned or challenged, integrity gives us a foothold to stand on. The Bible describes Satan as the accuser of the brethren[25] and though he may have something to accuse us of because we have all sinned and have all fallen short of the glory of God,[26] there is no condemnation for us in Christ.[27] We are now the righteousness of God through Christ Jesus[28] and we should live a life of integrity because integrity and truth cannot be separated, just like truth and love cannot be separated. So, what does that mean for us? Choosing to walk in integrity means walking in both truth and righteousness.

It is only when we walk in integrity that we can truly build in excellence.

Put it into Action!

1. In what areas of your life are you not practising integrity? And what can you do differently today to make sure that you're living a life of true integrity?

2. When was the last time you felt you compromised your integrity? What caused it and what lesson are you taking from that situation to apply to your life now?

CHAPTER FIVE

The Love of
an Excellent Builder

It's important to note that to build in excellence is to build in love. Why? Because everything that God has ever done has been excellent and everything that God has ever done has been in love because He is love[1].

There are so many ways in which you can build in love. Some are obvious whilst others not so much. There are some ways that I believe are extremely important but are probably not what first come to mind when you think about building in excellence.

Love

So, what is love? Why is it important? And what does this have to do with building? Well, the Bible teaches us that God is love and those who love, have been born of God and know Him.[1] We are reminded that because God loved us, we ought to love one another.[2] In fact, Jesus' commandment to His disciples was that they love others in the same way that He loved them, and in doing so, others will know that they were sent by Jesus Himself.[3]

Love is a trademark of the lovers of God. We are distinguished by our love, and it is an expression of Him because He is love[1]. In Apostle Paul's letter to the Corinthian church, he outlines the characteristics of love so that they (and the world at large) could identify it amongst all the other expressions of love in the world.

Love is patient and kind; love does not envy or boast; it is not arrogant or rude. It does not insist on its own way; it is not irritable or resentful; it does not rejoice at wrongdoing but rejoices with the truth. Love bears all things, believes all things, hopes all things, endures all things. Love never ends.[4]

Practically, this means that in every aspect of our building, be it via our communication with potential clients, your marketing strategy, or your prayer life, you need to live out love as we see it in the Bible. Love is not an option but it is a command[5] and we ought to obey it because that in itself, is a demonstration of love.[6]

Keep in mind that obedience is a demonstration of love. I believe it's important to understand that whenever you obey God's instruction, in any capacity, you are loving Him and also loving His people directly or indirectly. The more you obey, the deeper you walk in love. Through your obedience, you are demonstrating your trust in God and are allowing yourself to co-labour with God to build something in excellence.

So, let's look deeper into some ways we can actually build in love, shall we?

Humility

The Merriam-Webster dictionary defines humility as 'not [being] proud or haughty; not arrogant or aggressive.' The Cambridge University Press defines humility as 'tending to consider yourself as having no special importance that makes you better than others. Though these are helpful definitions of humility, I don't think they fully capture it's meaning.

In Andrew Murray's Book, *Humility: The Beauty of Holiness,* he beautifully explains what humility truly is: *Nothing is more natural and beautiful than to be nothing, that God may be all.* And the best person to demonstrate this is our Lord Jesus Himself. In Paul's letter to the church of Philippi, he encourages them to think of themselves the way Christ Jesus thought of Himself.[7] He gently reminds them that though Jesus had an equal status with God, He set aside the privileges of His deity and took on the form of a mere human being. But it doesn't end there, Jesus lived this out in obedience even to the point of death on the cross.[8]

Paul wasn't saying that Jesus desired the attention in His heart but rather fought against the desire, pushed through and decided to appear humble. Jesus truly humbled, and lowered Himself in obedience to God, for our sake. To put this into perspective, imagine trying to bring the fullness of the sky and condensing it into a grain of dust-sized container, can you even imagine that? The Creator of the universe,[9] the one in whom the fullness of the Godhead dwells,[10] decided to become a man - whose life was nothing but a faint whisper, a mere breath.[11] What a beautiful thing.

Humility also requires putting your ego aside, which is your desire to be self-sufficient, and actually seeking help. We'll explore the importance of not being a lone wolf builder in later chapters, but for now, remember that sometimes you need to look to the heavens and like David wrote in Psalm 121, ask yourself, from where does my help come from?[12] If your answer is not from the Lord, who made the heavens and the earth,[13] then you need to ask God to help you find your way back to the point where He is your primary source of help. Sometimes, you will lose sight of this and like I do, trust in yourself or other external things but the key thing when you realise that this has happened to you is to turn back, recalibrate, refocus, and reenergise. God's supply of help is unlimited, and believe me you'll never lack as long as God is your help.

Serving

When you are building in excellence, it can be so easy to get caught up in what you need and what you're doing, that you can forget that others are also in need of your support. Serving others and using your gifts, talents, and resources to help them allows you to truly appreciate the work of God in their life first hand.

Seeking and Accepting Feedback

You're neither perfect nor do you have it all together on this journey. I've said it many times before but I'll say it again. In order to grow and develop, regardless of what part of the journey you are on, you need to be willing and eager to receive feedback, and challenge from other people.

Just like I would help you identify your blind spots as a life coach which in turn will help you heal and grow, you need to be willing to let those around you highlight your blind spots through constructive feedback. Initially, this may seem intimidating and you may take feedback personally but with time, you'll quickly realise its importance and notice that not everyone who gives you feedback is trying to 'take you down'. To be honest you don't want yes men either.

A few years back, I worked as a career coach for young people which involved daily one-on-one and group coaching sessions. A significant part of my day however, involved giving and receiving feedback from team members including managers. At first, I found it quite difficult, as I was often thinking *who am I to give feedback to my manager?* Other times I thought I was not qualified to be in this role, let alone give feedback to someone who's been doing this role for years. Though this sheds light on some of my insecurities and unhealthy thought patterns, after giving feedback to others multiple times a day, five days a week, month after month, it became possible and even desirable. I noticed a rapid growth in my coaching abilities and in my ability to provide feedback to my team members, the young people I coached, and external partners.

This perspective on feedback completely revolutionised the way I went about my day-to-day living, from my development at work, right through to my relationships. I remember I once asked my friends how I could be a better friend; their responses were such eye-openers and though some responses may have been hard pills to swallow, they definitely helped me to see things that I wouldn't have noticed by myself and also affirmed in me those qualities that I overlooked or even frowned upon. I now try to constantly seek feedback regarding anything I may be doing e.g., coaching or YouTube videos. I can do this for the little and bigger things because I am confident that the people whom I'm seeking feedback from, have my best interest at heart and their thoughts and opinions shared are ultimately for my benefit.

Seeking and accepting feedback isn't a new thing, and it isn't just part of the rising personal development movement. It has been around since the day Adam and Eve ate from the Tree of the Knowledge of Good and Evil. Their decision to eat from that tree was their way of saying, 'I know what God has said but I know better', and we all know that by experience alone, we don't know as much as we think we do. In the Bible, God tells us that His thoughts are nothing like our thoughts and that His ways are far beyond anything we could ever imagine.[14]

Thinking that we know better than God is pride, and that's what got Satan kicked out of Heaven.[15] When we choose to live for God, we have to constantly search, our minds, thoughts, feelings, emotions, and behaviours for pride and do what we can to get rid of it immediately. For example, confessing your sin friend and telling them actionable you have come up with ensure you are no longer walking in the unfruitful way so that they can hold you accountable. Biblically speaking, if you listen to advice and you are willing to learn, one day you will be wise.[16] So, what does that mean for you and I? That part of building in excellence requires you to put your ego aside and seek feedback. When we do this, excellence will flow naturally and wisdom will be our portion.

It's currently a Wednesday evening as I'm in my kitchen typing this chapter out. I actually thought I was almost done with this section but I was reminded of something. The night before I went live on Instagram with my friend and fellow life coach, we were exploring the topic of self-awareness and personal development and it was very refreshing. Whilst we were there, one of the questions that was asked was, 'What is the impact of self-awareness on your growth?' My answer involved the linking of our personal development journeys to that of a sprout becoming a full-grown tree. It takes time, but the more you know about yourself and within this context, the more you know about what you are trying to build but even more importantly, you know who you are building for and with that, you are able to understand what you need to stop, start and carry on doing. So remember, feedback is a tool for maturity, and a vital ingredient for growth.

To build in love is to sow in love, and if you sow in love you will reap in love.

Put it into Action!

1. Can you confidently say you are building and walking in the Love of God? Why?

2. What could you do differently in your building process that would mean you are walking and building in excellence?

3. What could you get feedback on? Who will you ask for it and how will you implement the feedback?

CHAPTER SIX

No Lone Wolves:
With God,
with People

First things first, you are not building alone. Ever. You are co-labouring with God. The brand that you are building is an idea from God that He has entrusted you with. He has also placed you in a community, that can offer the help and support you need to bring His vision to life and similarly, so that you can help bring God's idea into our physical realities.

It can be very easy to lose sight of God amidst all the planning, building and execution. In fact, there will be moments that you will lose sight of God, but there's hope. The reality is that you'll have to manage many other demands of life such as jobs, friends and family, so you'll need to incorporate the necessary disciplines to help you stay in the space of continuous co-labouring with God. These disciplines will help you to recalibrate and get back on track when you lose focus.

Building your brand according to Biblical principles is not only about having scriptures plastered all over your products and social pages, or using christianese (Christian jargon) in your captions (though there is nothing wrong with this); it goes beyond that. It is possible to build a faith-based brand in a way that is not pleasing to God but it's also possible to build a non-faith-based brand in a way that is pleasing to God. Your foundations are extremely important, and all the more so because they are built upon the foundations that you have in your own personal relationship with God.

Just because we are Christians doesn't mean our target audience must only be Christians. Actually, our target audience should be those who don't know the Lord because through our brands and business, we are letting our light shine before mankind so that they may see our good deeds and moral excellence, to also give glory to our God in heaven.[1] What we are doing is offering a revelation of God and an expression of ourselves.

Co-labouring with God within the context of building in excellence is simply living out a submitted life, and a dedicated life to Jesus, where you surrender to His will and move by His leading. How do we do this, you ask?

Apply the Word of God.

In Psalm 109, we read that the Word of God is a lamp onto our feet and a light unto our path.[2]

What scriptures are you going to assign to your brand? You can apply the Word of God to everything and anything. Don't just pick scriptures for the sake of doing so but ensure that you have prayerfully chosen your scriptures and that you are committed to living by them.

The Word of God stands forever. The Word of God is a lamp onto your feet. Don't neglect the Word but rather, ensure that it is engraved and embedded into your brand. Like I mentioned earlier, it doesn't need to be explicitly in your branding, but it definitely needs to be woven into all that you do, to and for it. When you're making business decisions, what scriptures can you hold on to when you're not sure? When you appear to be making a loss, what scriptures will you hold on to? When you're developing your mission or vision statement, what scriptures come to mind. Remember that building a brand or business requires all of you. It will require your emotional, mental, physical, social and spiritual strength, so the more of God's Word that dictates those areas of your life, the easier it will be to apply the Word of God directly to what you are looking to achieve through your brand.

Applying the Word of God is not just for the sake of being a good Christian entrepreneur, but so that you can continue walking in the path of righteousness, even in your calling as a builder.

Prayer

Praying in its simplest terms is to be in conversation with God. When we consider the intercession of Abraham over Sodom and Gomorrah in Genesis 18, that was a conversation. When Moses was pleading with God to have mercy on the children of Israel in Exodus 33, that too was a conversation. When Jesus was in the Garden of Gethsemane, praying the famous prayer, 'Lord not my will but yours,'[3] He was also in a conversation with God. We are encouraged to pray without ceasing, never stop praying, and constantly pray[4] and that's exactly what we need to be doing, regardless of whether we are working on our brands or not. In a chapter 1, I mentioned that one of my favourite quotes was 'communication breeds connection'. By Apostle Michael Orokpo, a Nigerian based preacher and pastor. To continue to build intimacy with God, we need to be in communication with Him, talking to Him, listening to Him, reading His Word and making every effort to know Him deeply and intimately. Some days, it may be harder to pray and on other days, it may be easier, but your purpose in this life is to know Him personally, so keep praying.

A conversation involves two or more people speaking and listening to each other. So, when you are praying, though it is important to make your requests known to God[5] and cast your burdens onto Him,[6] you need to harken your ears and heart to His voice. Listen to what God is saying to you because He is speaking, even in His silence; when your soul is quietened, you can hear Him clearly. Be still before the LORD and wait patiently for Him,[7] for He knows more about you and more about the brand or business you are building than you do. He knows every single detail and He wants to share it with you, so pray and listen also.

I liken the prayers we pray about the vision God has given us, to prayers of dedication. More times than not, we're probably asking God what to do next, how to overcome an obstacle, or for creative direction. In doing this, what you are communicating to God is that, He can continue to trust you with this vision because, He is not only at the heart of it all, but at the beginning and the end of your journey too. You're acknowledge that this is His idea in your hands, so you are merely a steward of God's gift to the world. You are surrendering your will and giving Him full authority over the steering wheel.

You would have probably heard this before, 'unless the Lord builds a house, the builders build in vain.'[8] The message here is, don't try to go down a path unless the Lord has sent you there, and don't just start something unless the Lord is doing it with you otherwise, you'll quickly grow to realise that the sacrifices you have to make aren't worth it. So be sure to consult God about all your ideas, and ask Him which ones you should proceed with and how. Regularly check in with God, and you won't need to make any unnecessary sacrifices.

Previously, we explored the importance of reading the Word of God, and now we've just looked at the necessity of prayer. However, what I want us to look at now is the intersection between the two, which is praying with the Word. We already know that the Word of God is a light on our journeys, but the Word of God is also spirit and life.[9] God's Word is profitable for teaching and rebuking error, correcting faults and giving instruction for a righteous living.[10] Can you see what the fusion of the two produces? When we pray according to God's Word, we are doing exactly what Jesus encouraged us to do, which is to pray in spirit and in truth.[11] Pray with the Word, and by doing this, you will be continually transformed by the renewal of your mind, so that you may be able to discern what the true, perfect and acceptable will of God is[12] and then you will also find success in God.

Obedience

Jesus says that if we love Him, we will obey His Word.[13] This doesn't just refer to the ten commandments but it extends to those instructions we find in scripture such as extending grace and mercy to each other, [14] carrying each other burdens[15], not worrying[16], and being strong in the Lord[17]. It extends even further to those instructions that God has given to us personally. When you walk in obedience, you walk in love and when you walk in love, you build in excellence.

Obedience to God includes your desire to have control. It involves trusting in the Lord with all your heart and leaning not on your own understanding[18] and the fruits of doing so are sweet. In God's message to the rebellious people of Judah, He reminds them that if they are willing and obey Him, they will eat the best of the land.[19] When Jesus cast out a demon from a man who couldn't speak and was accused of getting His power from the prince of demons,[20] part of His response to the crowd was, 'Blessed are all who hear the word of God and put it into practice'.[21]

I could continue listing scriptures, but you get the point, because obedience is a win-win, and it gives God the space to fully be the Lord of your life you also enjoy the fruits of it. In every situation, fear the Lord and obey His commands.[22]

Okay, let's change the angle a little bit and explore the role of other people in our building process.

If you didn't know before, then you know by now that we are built and wired for relationship and community. By simply looking at the Godhead and observing how the Father, Son and Holy Spirit work, you'll realise that the Godhead is the model for relationship that we so desperately need. God will never ask us to do anything that He Himself has not done. So, He has not designed us to be in relationships and a community, if He hasn't modelled that Himself.

Just because we are not built to go through life alone doesn't mean that you should spend 24 hours of your day, and seven days a week with other people. You need time to yourself, especially since we are in a world where being 'booked and busy' is attractive. We need to be able to get away and find solitude. Even Jesus Himself retreated from the crowds numerous times to spend time with God. He had a habit of retiring to deserted places and praying.[23] We should also find a habit or retreating and spending intimate time with our Lord and friend.

I've always been an independent person, and part of it is natural, dare I say even genetic. But another part of it is that I'm the eldest of four children. I moved to this country when I was a little girl (but old enough to understand everything that was going on), and I'm also a Nigerian, from the Igbo tribe. So, I've always been one to simply just get on with it. If I don't know how to do something, I'll learn to figure it out. This isn't an inherently negative characteristic, as it's taught me a lot about 'grinding' and resilience. It means that I don't easily give up, I'm used to the perseverance and endurance Olympic games. This mentality has helped me to develop problem solving skills, take the initiative and promote innovation in all that I do. It's played a great role in my maturity.

The problem I usually faced was that having this 'I can do it myself' attitude meant that asking for help was often my last point of call. Though this wasn't the sole reason for my reluctance to seek help when needed, it still meant that there were some struggles and seasons of sufferings that I went through alone that I could have had a community to go through it with.

When I initially developed the Building in Excellence programme, there was a session dedicated to exploring Biblical stories that demonstrated what it meant to build in excellence in the right way. One of those stories was that of Moses and the building of the tabernacle and the temple. When he was given the instructions of how to build the temple and what resources would be needed, God told Him to go to the community of the children of Israel.

And Moses spoke to all the congregation of the children of Israel, saying, "This is the thing which the Lord commanded, saying: 'Take from among you an offering to the Lord. Whoever is of a willing heart, let him bring it as an offering to the Lord: gold, silver, and bronze; blue, purple, and scarlet thread, fine linen, and goats' hair; ram skins dyed red, badger skins, and acacia wood; oil for the light, and spices for the anointing oil and for the sweet incense; onyx stones, and stones to be set in the ephod and in the breastplate. All who are gifted artisans among you shall come and make all that the Lord has commanded'". [24]

Then everyone came whose heart was stirred, and everyone whose spirit was willing, and they brought the Lord's offering for the work of the tabernacle of meeting, for all its service, and for the holy garments. [25]

One of the key things I want to highlight from these scriptures is that, with every vision you have, God knows exactly what you need to bring it to fruition. And often times, the resources and help you need is not that far away. It shows that all that was required to build the space in which God's manifest presence would dwell, was within the same community He would dwell in. Isn't that wonderful! Everything Moses needed was within the community that he belonged to. You may be in a position where God has asked you to build a brand or business that is beyond your means, but be encouraged with these scriptures, as the Lord knows what you need and He will show you who and where to go.

Asking for help isn't the easiest thing to do and I know that well myself, but like I mentioned earlier, you are not supposed to build alone, because building in excellence means to build in a community. You don't know it all, nor can you do it all; your attempts to try and do things solo will push you into a dark hole of loneliness and will have you running around like a headless chicken, with no sense of direction or destination.

I'll show you what this looked like for me. One of my friends is part of a community that hosts various kinds of events throughout the year, so because I was in search of a venue to also host an event, instead of searching high and low for a venue, I reached out to him to ask if he knew any spaces that he thought would be good for me to use for my event. Another one of my friends is a baker, so I asked her if she could bake a cake for my event and she said yes! Another friend of mine had cousins who are photographers and videographers, so instead of worrying about how I was going to obtain professional photos by myself at home and edit them, I was able to work with both of them for a project. Instead of creating the logo for my personal brand, I reached out to a graphic designer, and it freed up some space in my mind to think about other things. My point is, a lot of the resources you need may be right under your nose. Sometimes, you may have to do a bit of looking and scouting to find what you need, but it's never too far away, as you might just have to go through a friend of a friend of a friend.

A quote by Barak Obama, former President of the United States says, '...Asking for help isn't a sign of weakness, it's a sign of strength. It shows you have the courage to admit when you don't know something, and to learn something new.' Don't let anyone or anything deceive you into thinking that asking for help shows incompetence or weakness, because if anything, it demonstrates humility and wisdom. So, the summary of this matter is, ask for help.

It's not just about asking for help, however that's important, it's about accountability and having people who are able to offer you advice when you may not even think that you need it. When the Israelites had escaped the Egyptians, Jethro, Moses' Father-in-law, went to visit Moses; when he saw the weight of the responsibility that Moses carried, leading the people of Israel, he couldn't help but to speak up. He said to Moses that his job was too heavy a burden to handle all by himself,[26] and he advised Moses to delegate, and train others up so that they could also carry part of the responsibility and ease the burden.[27]

We all need a Jethro in our lives, who not only points out the unhealthy behaviours in our lives but also offers us sound advice and wisdom. Think about how Moses' life would have looked like if he hadn't received that advice; he would have probably been burnt out, aged faster and who knows, maybe the children of Israel may have spent longer than forty years in the wilderness.

When I was writing this book, I knew I needed to develop a greater discipline for writing, and in order for me to do this, I needed accountability. So, I messaged my friend and told her that for one month, I would write every day (except Sundays, as that's my Sabbath) and text her once I'm done. I mentioned that my goal was to finish the first draft of this book as soon as possible. So, no excuses were allowed, except for some reason where I had lost the ability to use my hands (praise God that was never the story). I love accountability, because it's not just about telling someone to make sure you do something but it's an act of love. Through accountability, you are able to support someone's journey of building in excellence and vice versa.

To wrap this section up, love God, obey God, and labour with Him and remember, you are building in excellence, both with God and with people.

Put it into Action!

1. In what ways are you hoarding control and not co-labouring with God in your building process?

2. What can you implement in your routine this week that will allow you to build with God and with people?

3. Who within your community can hold you accountable to building in excellence?

CHAPTER SEVEN

The Principled Builder

You live by principles whether you're aware of them or not. By identifying these principles you desire to live by, you can integrate excellence into your way of living without having to work overtime. Having studied the way language can be used to change the way the brain processes information and consequently alter behaviour, it wouldn't be right for me to write a whole book about excellence and not include anything about principles. Thus, in this chapter, I'll share some of my foundational principles. These principles have had the biggest impact on my life and I've decided to live by them every single day.

1. There are lights at night

It was an ordinary spring evening, I had just finished off at work and decided to go on a walk by the river, to simply clear my head. It was golden hour; the sky was a toasted orange and the waters twinkled like the stars at night. As I played the role of a landscape photographer and tried to capture what only human eyes could perceive, I decided to write a poem about a revelation I had received in the weeks that had just gone by. It was titled, "Sun Rise" and it went a little bit like this:

In my life,
I've seen the sun set
I've seen the night

I've been living in the night.

My world seemed to be asleep
So, I tried to wake up my world and failed
I tried to fly across to another world
A world where I hoped there'd be light.

But what I had failed to see was that
In the night the stars are bright
And that there is infact
Light in the night.

He made lights to govern the day
He made lights to govern the night
And though my world seemed darker than what I hoped for
He showed me the light.

Slowly, slowly indeed but surely,
I began to see the lights,
The many lights he had placed in the firmaments of my world
I finally began to see the beauty of the night

And only then did I begin to see,
The sun rise.

Life isn't always filled with rays and sunshine. Life isn't easy and it doesn't take an intellectual to know this. Even a young child is aware of the state of our world. There was a five-year period in my life where my world seemed to be in a permanent state of darkness. There didn't seem to be any hope for light, and even if there was, it was quickly snuffed out.

What I wrote in that poem captured one of my learnt lessons and is now a principle I apply every day without fail; I try to see the lights at night. Even in the darkest valleys, even when there seems to be no hope, we need to make a conscious effort to see the light. Even in the small things such as when I am frustrated because I've missed the bus or because my dad has eaten the food I left in the fridge, I have to choose to see the light in those situations and sometimes, it looks like simply breathing in and out, counting to ten and reminding myself that God is bigger, and God is better and greater than anything I'm experiencing at the moment. I'm not saying you shouldn't allow yourself to feel, no, that's far from that. There is a time to weep and a time to laugh. A time to mourn and a time to dance.[1] There is also a time to sit in your emotions but in the moments when you don't need to, when sitting in your emotions will do more damage than good, this is when you need to find the light the most.

I understand this may not be easy, but believe me, I too have been in situations where I've been told to still have hope but I was thinking, 'Do you even understand?' The good news is that God understands. When Job lost everything, he fell face down, tore his rob, shaved his head and worshiped God saying, "Naked (without possessions) I came [into this world] from my mother's womb, and naked I will return there. The Lord gave and the Lord has taken away; blessed be the name of the Lord."[2] When Shadrach, Meshach and Abednego refused to bow down to King Nebuchadnezzar's golden statue and were sentenced to death by the fiery furnace, they said, "If the God we serve exists, then he can rescue us from the furnace of blazing fire, and he can rescue us from the power of you the king. But even if he does not rescue us, we want you as king to know that we will not serve your gods or worship the gold statue you set up."[3]

Whatever the situation, choose to find the light; it's always there even if you can't see it. Feel it, if you can't feel it, listen to it and if you can't hear it, hold fast to the truth that it's there - He is there. God is pure light[4] and if you believe what He says that He will personally go ahead of you. [That] He will be with you; He will neither fail you nor abandon you,[5] then you will find the light sooner or later.

More specifically with building a brand in excellence, there will be highs and lows and there be hurdles and road blocks, but remember that all things work together for the good of those who love Him and are called according to His purpose.[6] So, even in those frustrating moments, choose to find God's handprint, His voice, or His footsteps. In doing so, you'll see the light that will brighten your path.

2. Be Still

There's something about being still that is so powerful. No wonder it's not just a Christian practice. It is something that is embedded into the growing new-age of spirituality, mindfulness, and other self-help solutions. Life is full of noise; the world never stops moving, and life never stops. Everything just carries on; the clock continues to tick and nothing can pause time for anyone or anything. And now in our society, where busyness is commended and often mistaken for productivity, where work from home has blurred the boundary between work and personal life, where the pressure to be on the property ladder, financially free and living 'your best life' all before thirty years is ever growing, it doesn't seem like there's much time to stop and be still.

When I've been on the go for too long, I often find myself saying that I need time and space to breathe. Sometimes life can feel suffocating and that's not necessarily a bad thing as it happens. But what's important is how you ensure that you are well prepared for those seasons and how you can recover from those seasons if they end up knocking you down.

Stillness

A very popular scripture goes like this, 'Let be, be still, and know (recognise and understand) that I am God. I will be exalted among the nations! I will be exalted in the earth![7] For us, especially in modern society, we need to be able to take intentional moments to be still and realise that God is exactly who He says He is. He's a healer,[8] a defender,[9] a restorer,[10] a father,[11] a friend[12] and so much more.

I realised the importance of stillness even more so whilst I was in the process of writing this book, starting my masters degree, building my coaching career etc. So, I decided to carve out at least 10 minutes every day to just be still. This was not prayer, it was not reading my Bible, it was not a time to think about the worries of life, but to simply be still and know that He is God. And not only that, but to truly believe in that. Sometimes, I would play sounds of streams of water in the background to help me get into that space. I wasn't rigid with this, so on some days, I would do it in the morning after I'd gotten ready or I would do it during the day or even in the evenings, as and when needed.

At first, it was extremely challenging; it put into perspective how much was going on in one's mind and how it's always active. What I found most shocking was how slow those 10 minutes felt. I treasured and I still do treasure those pockets of time in my day, because I always felt so refreshed coming out of those 10 minutes and sometimes, I felt I needed more time and where possible, I would extend my time. As time went on, I realised that despite the intensity of my life, I was secure and I wasn't overwhelmed. Though I would still feel anxious and stressed out at times due to external situations, I knew that I just needed to be still and remember, *Marthina God's Got you, and he's got you covered.* Whenever I panic, whenever I'm worried or overwhelmed, I take a few seconds to just stop, take a deep breath in, take a deep breath out, and be still.

Being still recalibrates your mind. It helps you focus on those necessary things.

3. Take Things Step by Step

I know God can call you to do something with urgency even if you have no idea of what you're doing. For example, He might give you a message, ask you to record a video and upload it to your new YouTube channel or give you an instruction to start a business when your finances are seemingly moving the wrong way. God is not limited to or bound by anything. When He asks you to do something that seems completely impossible by what you see and are surrounded by, take it as another opportunity for God to show His glory in your life to do the miraculous, and the impossible. However, in that same breath, God may give you a similar vision, but the instructions come as you go forward.

If God has given you the instruction to build a business, start a blog or social media page, then you need to pay close attention and be intentional about what you do between now and then i.e., between the conception of the idea, to its execution and beyond. For every different person and vision, the journey from conception to execution will look different. Either way, the first thing you need to do is to ask God what He wants you to do and what your focus should be. You must surrender your will to Him and let Him direct your path.

When I work on a project of any kind, I tend to follow a process that allows me to smoothly (at least it helps me attempt to) execute the vision. Here's an example.

One night, in the latter half of 2019, I had just finished praying and I suddenly felt a surge of inspiration to start planning the production of a podcast, so I began my personalised process in building a brand; I established my why, I conducted my market research, I planned logistics and episodes, I created a timetable for when to record, edit and release, I created the logo for the Instagram page and all the other content I deemed necessary. This process did not start and end that night, but it took weeks and months. I did what I knew I could and needed to do at the time and I held on to this project with the hope of taking it out of my secret place and presenting it to the world.

For over four years, I waited for God to tell me what to do next. I was aware that He could ask me at any time to change the name, the branding, etc. So, I was always keeping an ear and eye out for that. But also, over the years, I had learned so much that the glimpse of the vision I was given could look much different now because I had grown in knowledge and experience. I was so certain that this vision would materialise so much that I even began prepping for future collaborations and development points (when there was nothing to work with).

Though I thought I was ready to execute my plan, God had more lessons He wanted to teach me. He showed me the importance of taking things step by step; I have no issue with running with a vision (my friends know how many 'visions' I've run with), but my problem is that, my zeal to see it come to fruition can sometimes blind me so I miss some important lessons along the way.

A Chinese proverb and one of my all-time favourite quotes by Philosopher Lao Tzu says, 'A journey of a thousand miles begins with just one step'. This was one of the means through which God taught me the life-changing lesson about pace, by taking things step by step.

When I think about what God has called me to do, and I look even closer at the tasks that he has revealed to me for the present or near future, it's often intimidating. Yes, it can also be exciting but it's always beyond my scope and more than anything I can do on my own (which is a good sign in my opinion, as it's an opportunity to let God show His glory to the world by doing the impossible through and in you).

Time and time again, I would find myself asking God, 'But how? Where do I even begin?' and I've realised that the answer to that question is Him. Our journeys ought to begin, continue, and finish in Him. Whether it's starting a business God has placed in your heart or learning how to play an instrument, whether it's starting a blog page or beginning the journey of switching career paths, you must always start in Him. Talk to Him and listen to Him too, because God will instruct you on what your next course of action should be. I don't believe that there is such a thing as too little of a prayer. God cares about everything that relates to you, and though there may be times when some things take priority over others, it's important to stay rooted and hidden in Christ.

God demonstrates this even in His creation of what is our present realities, life. God didn't create everything in one day, nor did He create everything at the same time. He created the world and six days later he created human beings, and in between that time, He created birds, fish, land animals, plants, and much more. God didn't just create Moses and drop Him off at Pharaohs palace, but in the book of Exodus, we see step by step, the development of Moses as an individual and eventually, as a leader, sent to deliver the people of Israel from their oppressors, the Egyptians. Consider the process taken to build the tabernacle.

Bezalel made bars of acacia wood; five for the [frame] boards for one side of the tabernacle, five bars for the boards of the other side of the tabernacle, and five bars for the boards at the rear side to the west. And he made the middle bar pass through, [horizontally] halfway up the boards from one end to the other. He overlaid the boards and the bars with gold and made their rings of gold as holders for the bars.

Furthermore, Bezalel made the veil of blue, purple and scarlet fabric, and fine twisted linen; he made it with cherubim, the work of an embroiderer. For the veil (partition curtain), he made four support poles of acacia wood and overlaid them with gold; their hooks were gold, and he cast for them four silver sockets. He made a screen (curtain) for the doorway of the tent of blue, purple, and scarlet fabric, and fine twisted linen, the work of an embroiderer; and [he made] the five support poles with their hooks and overlaid their [ornamental] tops and connecting rings with gold; but their five sockets were bronze.[13]

This is just a fraction of the entire tabernacle construction, and look at how many different parts there are! Building this tabernacle, and other things including the covenant box, involved taking things one step at a time, to ensure that everything was completed to the blueprint that God had given to them. It didn't happen overnight either, but this involved multiple steps over a period of time and eventually, a beautiful sanctuary for the Lord to dwell in was created.

This principle applies to every area of your life, so decide to take things one step at a time. Each step will look different; some easier to take than others, some bigger than others, and likewise, some smaller than others. Some seasons involve you taking lots of little steps whilst other seasons involve you taking a minimal number of large steps. Sometimes, you don't move for a while and other times you are constantly on the go. Now and again, you may know the next steps to take and more often than not, you will need to take steps of faith meaning that, even though you don't know the next steps, you'll move anyway because you know and believe that your steps are ordered by the Lord, so you have nothing to be afraid of. This book is a physical reminder for me and should also be an encouragement and serve as a testament to you that sometimes, good things take time and lots of steps. This book involved me taking lots of little steps and huge leaps to complete. Some steps seemed unnecessary, and some steps seemed ridiculously impossible but with every step, I was reminded that when God is involved, I ought to expect above and beyond all I could ever imagine.

Remember, it's a journey so you'll meet many people along the way. You'll meet people who are about to take the same step as you, others who have taken the step you are due to take, and some whom you can advise because you have taken the step they are looking to take. Embrace the journey, and find the pockets of joy along the way. It may not always be easy but you are more than capable to do it for He has graced you to do that which He has called you to do. So, as long as you remain in Him and He in you, He will complete that good work which He has begun in you.[14] At the end of the day, He will take all the glory.

Put into Action!

1. What principles are you going to begin putting into practice today?

2. Are there any principles that you are living by that are hindering you from building in excellence?

CHAPTER EIGHT

The Excellent Steward

I remember a few years ago when I was delivering the Building in Excellence programme, I would always encourage the participants to see their brands as their own child—a product of themselves.

I can't quite remember whether it was a sermon at church, a YouTube video or a podcast that I was listening to, but it was through a conversation I was listening to or involved in myself that what I call, 'The Baby Perspective' came about. The premise for this perspective is that, you approach the process of building a brand in excellence in a similar manner to that which a parent would approach raising their new-born child.

You're probably familiar with the phrase, 'carbon copy', commonly used when a child is very similar to one or both of their parents. When you see the carbon copy child in close proximity with the parent, though they are two separate entities, and two separate individuals, you are able to tell that they are both very closely related. It's obvious and doesn't take much digging to come to this conclusion. Similarly, you as an individual are not your brand (even if you have a personal brand), yet, when someone identifies you and your brand, they should be able to immediately see how you and your brand are 'related'. Your eyebrow may still be raised and you may not be sure where this is all going but just stay with me for a moment.

In the same parent-carbon-copy-child context, naturally if a child looks like their parent, then they carry similar physical characteristics i.e., facial features. But one could also assume that they also carry similar behavioural characteristics. Laura Baker, an associate professor at the University of South Carolina, wrote an article about the role of genes in behaviour and found that genes influence each individual's behavioural and psychological characteristics.[1] So, we as the parent, play a role in passing on certain characteristics to our brands — our carbon copy. When you begin to see that your internal mental structures, value systems and beliefs can automatically be translated into your brand without you having to do any additional labour, you'll be able to understand why you need to ensure that you are internally building yourself excellently, so that you can build a brand, up in excellence.

Since adopting this perspective, I've noticed a positive, yet dramatic change to the way that I approached brand building. Whether it was starting my YouTube channel, building my personal brand or even writing this book, the Baby perspective forced me to take a deeper introspective look at myself and identify the positive value systems and beliefs that I held that I'd like to 'pass onto my child'. Equally, I had to humble myself and identify those limiting beliefs and victim mindsets that I had that I didn't want my brand to inherit. The good news is that, our brands are not literal children so we actually have greater control over what values and belief systems they are built on and 'inherit'.

Ultimately, if you are not passionate or burdened by a particular value, principle or cause in your own personal life, then you'll find it difficult to exercise this whilst building your brand. For example, if I wasn't in any way interested in pursuing excellence in my personal life, then it would be extremely difficult for me to even attempt to build a brand with its foundations on excellence. Think about it, if that were the case, this book would not be in your hands. Some people may argue that you can 'learn on the job' but that's not what this is, because when you are trying to build something by principles and values that you don't adhere to in your personal life, it breeds ground for ingenuity, and pretence, which will eventually come to light. That is exactly what we are trying to avoid; there may be some characteristics that you may want to develop and build your brand with. That is perfectly okay, and you will grow and develop in the process of the building, but what I'm getting at is, don't try and build your brand on foundations that aren't yours. Be authentic, be real and be honest; check yourself and move from there.

When I began building my YouTube channel, I remember making notes of some key values and principles I wanted to convey. They included open-mindedness, honesty, integrity and authenticity. These were characteristics that I strived to live by in my personal life, relationships, work ethic etc. Though these would naturally reveal themselves in the conversations on my channel, I tried to think of other ways to further amplify these qualities. That's when group discussions came to mind; I would often have group discussions or get viewers to send in their thoughts, questions and opinions on certain topics, which I would delve deeper into during my videos. In this way, I felt I was demonstrating that I didn't think I was one who knew everything but valued the opinions of others. I shared my opinions on various subject areas and I made sure to never make my opinions and interpretations appear factual. In short, living out these values on my YouTube channel was more exciting and natural because it was coming from an extension in my own life.

The Baby Perspective is proactive; it's not enough to just be aware of this perspective, so I'd encourage you to live by it. The action part is: *what are you doing to raise your child in the way of the Lord?* The Bible tells us that children are a gift from God,[2] so in the same manner, you are to view the brand you are building, and the vision you are turning into a reality, as a gift from God also. When you really think about it, you didn't earn it or deserve it, but God in His loving kindness gave you this idea. All of this speaks of something called, **stewardship.**

To be a steward means to supervise arrangements or manage another's property. Stewardship in any capacity says a lot about you as an individual and speaks loudly of your character. Our lives are a test of stewardship, and even Jeremiah recognised that our lives are not our own,[3] so we are to be like good managers of God's different gifts,[4] and serve each other well with the life that we have been given.

When God created Adam and Eve, He placed them in the garden of Eden and He gave them dominion or rather, a responsibility to look after the fish, cattle livestock and over the entire earth.[5] From the beginning of time, we as human beings have been give the role of a steward. We have a responsibility to look after the planet we live on, and take care of the animals and plants of the earth. This was the original intent that God had for mankind. The responsibility bestowed on Adam and Eve was not to be fulfilled from a place of obligation or forced labour, but from a place of intimacy with God. They lived in such union with God that they heard the Lord walking in the Garden.[6] They looked after the land from a place of love and communion; that's the context through which stewardship should be sustained. So, whether it is your finances, relationships or gifts and talents, remember that stewardship is not something that somehow finds itself on your to do list, but it's something that comes naturally to you because it is an overflow of your communion with God.

Now that the table has been laid, let's look at some ways that stewardship can look like in our lives.

1. Your body

I remember when God asked me how I could be a faithful steward of the ideas He had given me, if I wasn't even able to faithfully take care of my body. I've had a not-so-smooth journey with my health in the last years (but we're healed now; glory to Jesus!) and that has had a huge toll on my self-care or rather self-maintenance.

Remember, your body is a temple of the Holy Spirit. You are not your own [property][7] so, you have a responsibility to manage the property that you have been gifted to look after. This means making sure that you are eating enough and eating the right kinds of food. It means giving your body the fluids it needs, exercising, sleeping enough etc. Often times when life becomes so difficult, we often neglect taking care of our bodies and that I can definitely confirm, has been my story one too many times. But I now realise the importance of eating, sleeping, and ultimately living well so I have put measures in place to help me stay on top of my bodily care, when the demands of life become excessive.

We are all at different stages in life, and though our bodies all have the same bodily functions, our bodies still function differently, regardless of where you are at. Ask God to highlight the ways in which you can best take care of His temple, which is your body.

2. Faithfulness

In Paul's letter to the Church at Corinth, He explained that he and Apollos have been put in charge of explaining God's mysteries,[8] and that it is required of stewards that they be found faithful.[9] Faithfulness can be defined as being true to one's word or commitments, when you chose to follow Christ, and you gave Him the right to be Lord over your life. In doing so, you submitted to His Lordship. Faithfulness is an expression of love and integrity, which are characteristics of an excellent steward. Choosing to be faithful, and loyal to Jesus means that you have consciously and are subconsciously making decisions that will please Him and as a result of that, you are taking care of the things He has placed in your care.

3. Your Money

This is a very tricky one, especially because money, finances and everything in between, is a very sensitive topic in the church. We've already established that our lives are not our own and they belong to God, so we are to be faithful stewards of the gifts that God has given us and use it to serve each other.[10] The same thing applies to your money; it does not belong to you, and in fact, it's provision that the Lord has left in your care, and He can ask you to invest it somewhere else whenever He pleases.

As someone who has experienced life as an employee and an entrepreneur, the way you view your money is a deal breaker. The way you view your financial behaviour is also a deal breaker. Is saving an act driven by fear of a lack of security in the future? Do you see spending money on certain goods and services as an expense, or a loss, instead of an investment in yourself and your future? Think about these questions and answer them truthfully.

It's easy to think that having more money may solve our problems and this is true to an extent; for example, if you've got a mountain of bills to pay, finding a way to get more money may well be the answer to clearing those bills. However, we operate at a different level as believers, because God requires us to be faithful stewards of the money that He has left within our care. So sometimes, God will train you and prepare you with what you have until you are ready to move on to the next level. Just like your gifts are to be used to serve others, so are your finances. Now, before anyone comes and starts giving out all their cash without any wisdom, and says it was Marthina who said this or that, I want to make it clear that the way in which God wants you to manage your finances will look different to your friends, leaders or mentors. At the end of the day, if Jesus came today and asked you to give a report on how you managed the investments He gave you, He should be saying 'Well done, my good and faithful servant. You have been faithful in handling this small amount, so now I will give you many more responsibilities.[11] The greater your finances, the greater your responsibility over it.

Like Paul, I know what it feels like to be in need and what it feels like to have more than enough.[12] It's a very privileged yet humbling set of experiences to have, yet in all circumstances, I've learnt the importance of letting go and trusting God with your money. Especially, in a society that is being crippled by a cost-of-living crisis, where the cost to live comfortably is increasing yet the source of income isn't increasing, it can be very difficult not to worry.

A common scripture that is quoted when someone says they have worries (not just specific to their finances), is found in Matthew 6, where Jesus encourages us to look at the birds in the sky and the grass on the fields. He reminds us that their daily needs are met, so how much more of us who are His children, and sheep in His pasture. There is so much to say on this topic and there are many sermons, podcasts, teachings, videos and research articles out there that can help you to understand God's will for your finances, so do your due diligence to search and understand this more. But for the sake of this book, the focus is on trusting that the God who cares about you holistically, also cares about your finances too. Remember, you are not your source of wealth. The Lord your God gives you the power to gain wealth.[13] Ask God to show you what trusting Him with your finances looks like, and once you do this, you'll find that you are on the path of being a faithful steward, and excellent steward of your finances.

4. Your Brand

Finally, Marthina!

I was saving this for last because I wanted to emphasise on the fact that building in excellence starts from within and pours out into all that you do. Being a faithful steward of your brand means that you take care of it and provide it with the nutrients it needs to grow. This could be investing in a course that would help build your skills, or networking with others to gain some 'parenting tips'. You should pray for your brand and apply the Word of God in every way that you can. Adopt 'The Baby Perspective' and show your brand the tender, loving, care that it needs to flourish in excellence, but remember, it starts first with you, but more specifically, it starts in you.

Put it into Action!

1. What practices do you have in place to ensure you are looking after your *baby*?

2. How are you managing what God has asked you to steward?

3. What do you need to do this week to be a better steward?

CHAPTER NINE

The Idolatry of Excellence

You must not have any other god but me. You must not make for yourself an idol of any kind or an image of anything in the heavens or on the earth or in the sea. You must not bow down to them or worship them, for I, the Lord your God, am a jealous God who will not tolerate your affection for any other gods. I lay the sins of the parents upon their children; the entire family is affected—even children in the third and fourth generations of those who reject me. But I lavish unfailing love for a thousand generations on those who love me and obey my commands.[1]

Idolatry is so much of a big deal that it's part of the ten commandments and is mentioned over 100 times in scripture. You probably don't have a huge golden calf sitting in your bedroom, but that doesn't mean you aren't committing or haven't committed idolatry.

Idolatry, according to Google, refers to the worship of idols or extreme adoration, love or reverence for something or someone. Hold fast to this definition as it will set the tone for this section. This whole book is focused on exploring the ways in which you can build in excellence, starting from the inside and then overflowing into your brands. We've looked at character development, the importance of integrity, love and so much more. But I would be doing you a great disservice if I didn't talk about the dangerous side of building in excellence. Because excellence highly demands of its wearer, it's not that difficult to idolise it. I'm not saying that you'll get a monument that says excellence or create a god of excellence, but I'm referring to the misdirection of worship.

The Google definition of idolatry is the extreme adoration, love or reference for something or someone. If Jesus is your Lord and personal saviour, it means He is the one that deserves all your love and adoration. David wrote in the Psalms, 'Ascribe to the Lord the glory due his name; worship the Lord in the splendour of holiness'.[2] A common theme through the Psalms was adoration and the glorification of God. We don't worship God because we're told to, but because He is worthy and deserving of it all.

God is a jealous God[3] and rightfully so. God created you so you would be in constant communion with Him. You are created for Him, and it is Him that is always at work in you, to make you willing and able to obey His own purpose.[4] He is your source of life,[5] your sustenance and the one who meets all your needs,[6] so He should be the core of your life, and the one who gets your full attention. However, despite reading, seeing and even experiencing the power of God, it's still possible to lose sight of Him.

Often times, the biggest temptation is just the demands of life. Balancing it all can be hard and when we are unable to do so, we often get our priorities wrong, and God is no longer in His rightful place at the top. In fact, it's important that we are aware that there is such thing as the idolatry of excellence, because then, we are able to identify it in its early stages and quickly adjust ourselves where necessary. Unlike obedience that bears fruit, idolatry bears no fruit, and it brings about confusion, and shame. Many things will try to take the place of God in your life, but it is your responsibility to make sure that God stays first above all things in your life. Thankfully, you aren't living life in your own strength, because you have been given the gift of the Holy Spirit who will guide you in all Truth.[7] He will help you walk in the right path that is pleasing to God.

So, how do we identify the idolatry of excellence? Here are three ways you can identify it.

First, if your pursuit of excellence is self-glorifying, then you are heading towards the road of idolatry, if that isn't the case already. The story of the tower of babel in Genesis chapter 11 demonstrates this perfectly.

And they said to one another, 'Come, let us make bricks and bake them thoroughly.' So, they used brick instead of stone, and tar instead of mortar. 'Come,' they said, 'let us build for ourselves a city with a tower that reaches to the heavens, that we may make a name for ourselves and not be scattered over the face of all the earth.'[8]

The individuals building this tower were skilled and talented such that they could have used their gifts for many other things, but they decided to build a city tower with the intention of making a name for themselves. We are called to do everything to the glory of God[9] and not to make a name for ourselves. We are to use the gifts we have to serve others[10] and worship God. So, what was the consequence for the people? They became confused and scattered. God Himself had to come and intervene, so He scattered them with a variety of languages and their attempts to build the tower was halted.[11]

This is not to say that you are not allowed to strive to build a network or acquire followers. The point is that, in all that you do, the glory of God to be revealed should be your aim, and if it's not then you know what to do...

Secondly, [regular] burnout. When I think about burnout in my journey of building in excellence, I'm taken back to the very early days of my coaching career (very humbling periods I must admit). I knew that in order to build my career as a coach, I needed to get some practice in before I could present myself publicly as a life coach. So, I asked some friends of mine if I could coach them; some for one-off sessions, and others for weeks or even months. As I was doing this, I sought and implemented their feedback on my coaching so that I was constantly developing. Whilst this was happening, I was running a weekly blog— a

YouTube channel that I posted to weekly. I was still a full-time university student with upcoming assignments and exams, and I also managed multiple social media pages for which I was responsible for creating and posting content. The list goes on. Though it was a very exciting period, as I was testing out this new career landscape, it was exhausting doing everything by myself. It wasn't until I could physically do nothing more that I realised that I pushed my mind and body to its limits. It affected my friendships, my studies and even my relationship with God.

For me in this instance, idolatry looked like taking matters into my own hands and doing everything by myself, neglecting my physical, mental and spiritual wellbeing, because I was afraid that if I didn't do these things then I wouldn't be doing everything that God called me to do and thus I'd be failing Him. By doing it myself, I was saying *Lord, I don't fully trust you can do this work through me.* Who am I and who are you to question God's ability. Though we may not understand or even know what to do, we need to remember that God's ways are above ours[12] and that in all circumstances, His plans for us are for good and not of evil.[13] So, we need to let go of control and trust that it will always work out with God.

Third and certainly not least, we must pray. We have already explored the importance of prayer in a previous chapter, but it's so important especially when we are dealing with idolatry. God isn't in the business of setting us up for failure; He wants us to prosper,[13] and those who delight in the teachings and instruction of the law are like trees that grow beside a stream and bear fruit at the right time...they succeed in everything they do.[14] Talk to God, and tell Him everything, including how you feel. Be honest, because He knows it all already but there's something about confession (not just of sin, but of emotions also) that is refreshing. He wants to hear what you have to say. God wants to talk to you also. He wants to tell you what's on His mind too, how He feels and what He wants to do.

It's a beautiful thing to have the privilege to develop a personal relationship with God, so cherish it and stay in a place of prayer at all times. It's in this place that the Lord will also reveal the ways in which you may be idolising excellence (if applicable) and it's in this same place that you will repent of your sin, and go boldly before the throne of grace.[15] He will forgive your sins and purify you from all your wrongdoings.[16] Pray always.

We have all fallen short of God's glorious standard[17] so don't be discouraged when you do stumble, because He's right by your side upholding you by His righteous hand.[18] Let him lead you on this journey, filled with highs and lows, and the knowns and the unknowns. It's all part of building in excellence.

Put it into Action!

1. In what ways, knowingly or unknowingly, have you idolised excellence?

2. What preventative measures can you put into place to help you, moving forward?

CHAPTER TEN

From My Community to You

I was thinking about how to finish this book and after deep thought, I felt inspired to reach out to my community (check me out, putting my words into action) and ask them two questions. The first is, 'What does Building in Excellence mean to you?' Secondly, 'What advice would you give to someone who is looking to start building in excellence?'

I'm so grateful to be surrounded by people who have a wealth of experience and wisdom. I've definitely been blessed by them and I'm confident that by sharing a glimpse of their knowledge and wisdom, you too will be blessed. So, thank you to everyone who contributed to my research. Your words will be nourishment to many people.[1]

As you read the answers to these questions, I encourage you to think about how you would use the knowledge you've obtained, to answer these questions. I also challenge you to send your answers to a friend, or even share it on your social media accounts. Now, you've got the foundations of what it means to build in excellence, so share it with others so that our communities can be full of excellent builders who build excellent things.

What does it mean for you to 'Build in Excellence'?

- Whenever I think about God building in the Bible, be it His creation or to inspire man to build a temple, it was excellent because of the precision and the detail. So, to me, building in excellence is about building with a strong understanding and context to do it precisely.

- To build in excellence is to strive towards the mark; to meet the end of the goal of something that is beautiful, edifying to others, and set apart from the rest.

- Me personally, this means to always try. Trying will get you to many places in life, so always try. Once you have tried, keep on trying. You may fall or you may break but that doesn't mean you have to stop trying. As all that effort you are making is building something so beautiful. You will simply be building in your own excellence, and no one can take that away from you. WHY? Simple, because you tried.

- It means to have a growth mindset founded on integrity, in order to achieve long-lasting results that go beyond oneself.

- To build in excellence means you are intentionally stewarding over things that you are working on and consistently trying to improve it!

- It means to consistently make good decisions.

- I think it means to build something to a high-quality service. Something that you would use the products/service.

- It means to build and grow something of standard and high quality.

- It means setting your mind on creating a project that gives a 360° value (for yourself, everyone around you, people you don't know, and even generations to come). Also, it means having a routine that brings out the most productivity in you to fully finish creating this project.

- To build in excellence is to adopt and nurture a culture of excellence as you grow.

- It means even from the planning stage, you plan a project to its very best potential. You don't limit potential of idea to current resource, personnel or connections.

- It means maintaining the highest standards when creating something.

- I believe building in excellence is you growing in all aspects of life. e.g., career, academic, spirituality etc.

- It means to build on a foundation of Christ with the Holy Spirit as your architect/manager. It means being diligent with the assignments given to you as part of your calling on Earth. It means to multiply your talents, not holding anything back because of fear. It implies leaving a legacy of integrity and transforming communities for the better.

- It means being delusional until you are what you aspire to be. The best way to build in excellence and become excellent I believe, is to convince yourself you can achieve anything you put your mind to even if you are nowhere near your goal. There is so much power in declaring excellence even when the path isn't clear, so much so that eventually, you will be surrounded with amazing people and opportunities that will continue to develop your excellence.

- For me, it means to build while being led by the Holy Spirit (who is the spirit of excellence). It means acknowledging that I don't know it all and in order for whatever vision, project, or idea I have to come to fruition, I should depend on God for the strategy and wisdom for it. Excellence is not perfection, but it is doing the best possible with the resources you have, whether that is time, money, people, giftings etc. In simple terms, it is building strategically with the strategy from God.

- Two scriptures come to mind when I think of Building in Excellence: the parable of the talents/three servants in Matthew 25:14-30 and the house built on rock in Matthew 7:24-28. Both scriptures are teachings that Jesus delivered to His disciples.

In the parable of the three servants, a master gave different portions of his money to his servants to take care of in his absence. When he returned from his long trip, he was delighted with the servants who invested his money and doubled it, but was appalled with the one who hid the portion he was given. This scripture presents the importance of using our gifts and skills to glorify God and not making half-hearted efforts to do so. Because God is excellent, we too should be excellent in building all areas of our lives for his glory, e.g., building healthy relationships with family and friends, building comprehensive understanding of the sectors we work in so we can widen our positive impact, etc. God however, isn't pressuring us to be excellent but instead, He wants us to come to this conclusion through our free will and divine revelation gently given to us. So, once we know this truth, we should strive to be excellent and take breaks when necessary to continue building excellence effectively and efficiently.

We are called to build in excellence but more so, to also build on Christ's teachings as a foundation to ensure the longevity of what we build. In the parable of the House built on rock, Jesus described those who listen to His teachings and put them into practice as people who build their house on rock rather than sand and are therefore unshaken by adverse events that life can throw at them. Keeping Jesus at the centre of our thoughts and actions will ground us and prevent what we build from being influenced by our shortcomings and perspective of life.

- Psalm 127:1 says that, 'Unless the LORD builds the house, he who builds labours in vain'.

Building in excellence starts with building according to God's will, God's leading, God's instruction, God's pattern, and God's principles. The world has a definition of building in excellence, but if you are building without God, then it is in vain, because although it may be excellent to a subjective worldly standard, it would not be pleasing to an objective Godly standard.

On a more practical level, I believe building in excellence involves establishing a culture around your idea, project or organisation with five key principles:

1. Consistency - persistence, continual effort, and endurance.

2. Time management - reliability, punctuality, and efficiency.

3. Honesty - openness, truth, and transparency.

4. Solution orientated mindset - optimism, and the ability to overcome challenges.

5. Quality control - high standards across the board; including planning process, suppliers, marketing, branding, production, delivery, and service.

I believe that a God ordained idea, project, or organisation built on these five principles is one that is built in excellence and destined to thrive!

If you could give one piece of advice to someone wanting to 'Build in Excellence' what would it be?

- Become an expert in your field!

- Have a good community of people around you who will push and challenge you, so that you can build in excellence.

- Do not give up, as excellence is something that comes from learning and making mistakes. But you must never stop; always strive for what you want and do not give up until you feel like you have achieved it. Once you take failure out of your head space, you will be building in excellence in no time.

- Start with consistency. Do one small thing consistently and add them up as you find your rhythm.

- Accountability is so important. Those around you who believe in what you're building and are always readily available to provide encouragement and faith watching documentaries of how others were able to build in excellence is very encouraging.

- Think long term, stay consistent, and keep pushing.

- They should build little by little and aim to try and improve with each step rather than for perfection.

- They should be authentic, patient and never compare themselves to anybody else's progress or achievements.

- They should think about how it will add value to the world.

- They should be observant; you have two eyes, two ears and one mouth. I believe you should watch and listen and question as much as you can so that when you speak, it is informed, thoughtful and considerate.

- Start as you mean to go on.

- Have a solid reason why and use other builders as templates.

- Be true to yourself and your project. Don't slack on what's necessary to be the best.

- I would recommend setting targets and goals and designing a roadmap for your future plans.

- Know your reason why. Building in excellence begins with a vision and that vision with great intention, can help someone to keep building even when they feel like giving up. Discipline comes from having a reason why.

- With everything you do, aspire to do it with maximum effort, so that when you look back at it, you know that you have put your all in to become the individual you aspire to be.

- There is only so much your skills and strengths can do so ask God for wisdom!

- I'd say, study Jesus and the former and latter prophets. Study how they carried themselves, how they interacted with God, how and when they rested, and how they worked. Jesus is my favourite example not only because He is God but because his instances of resting, retreating, and praying, as well are preaching, travelling, and communing are clearly written in the Bible. His story teaches us a wholistic example of how to build in excellence effectively.

- My advice would be to build with the right people backing you. First and foremost, is what you are building God-ordained? Do not build it unless GOD is backing you! But in addition to that, do not be afraid to build with people. Don't feel like you need to be the hero and do it all by yourself. Play to your strengths, but learn how to receive advice, mentorship, help, and also learn how to outsource, delegate, partner, and synergise with other people.

Epilogue

Back in 2020, I released a workbook which I created to be used to put into practice what was learnt in the Building in Excellence programme. So, when it came to writing this book, I thought it would simply be an extension of that workbook but as I began writing, I quickly realised God had very different plans. God simply wanted me to share what He had taught me over the years about building in excellence. At first, I was worried, I felt inadequate, and I felt that I had nothing to show for what it looked like to be Building in Excellence, but that was a lie from the enemy that I had to cast down.

Writing this book has been nothing short of both a challenging and rewarding journey; I have learnt so much about God and myself. It's funny because, this book is essentially me sharing the lessons that I have learnt over the last five years, yet in this process, it feels as though I've learnt more than I did in those five years. There were days when I was in the shower and on my knees, pleading to God for strength. There were days when my eyes were burning so much that I couldn't even open them because I was watching a screen all day at work and at home to get some writing done. There were days I was completely exhausted and I could write only but a couple of sentences and other days when I wrote thousands of words. There were days when I didn't believe it was possible to get this done and other days when I was so ready to be done; I was over it. There were good days and bad days but ultimately, God carried me through it all. He placed people around me who cheered me and lifted me up in prayer when I couldn't hold myself up. I've known God to be faithful, yet the journey of writing this book has revealed to me a deeper level of God's faithfulness that I'll cherish forever.

Building in excellence is a journey of a lifetime that never stops; you continue to learn and make mistakes but as long as you're doing it with God, you are in the right space, doing the right thing.

Once again, thank you for taking the time to read through the lessons I have learnt on my journey. I hope that you feel better equipped with the tools you need to live a lifestyle of excellence but even more so, that you are able to build your brands and businesses in excellence, so that the world may see your good works and give glory to the LORD our God in Heaven.

Your fellow builder,
Marthina Amarachi

Bibliography

Chapter 1: Miracles Whilst Building

1. 1 Kings 19:12 [NLT]

Chapter 2: Excellence Defined

1. Oxford Dictionary

2. Cambridge Dictionary

3. Merriam-Webster Dictionary

4. Matthew 5:14-16 [AMPC]

5. Titus 2:7 [TPT]

6. 1 Peter 2:9 [AMP]

7. Daniel 6:3 [ESV]

8. John 1:12 [GNT]

9. John 3:16 [GNT]

10. Philippian 2:13 [NLT]

11. Proverbs 22:29 [NKJV]

12. Esther 1:1-4 [NKJV]

13. Matthew 7:23 [MSG]

14. 1 Corinthians 10:31 [AMPC]

Chapter 3: The Character of an Excellent Builder

1. Matthew 9:9-13 [TPT]

2. John 4:9 TPT

3. John 4:4 [AMP]

4. John 4:39 [AMP]

5. James 1:2-4 [MSG]

6. Hebrews 12:11 [ESV]

7. Psalm 23:3 [NKJV]

8. Psalm 139:24 [NLT]

9. Romans 3:23 [ESV]

Chapter 4: Integrity: A Pillar of Excellence

1. Matthew 7:24-27 [TPT]

2. Jeremiah 17:9 [NKJV]

3. Luke 8:17 [NLT]

4. James 4:17 [NLT]

5. Matthew 6:8 [AMP]

6. Romans 8:27 [NEC/NTFE]

7. Romans 8:1 [CSB]

8. Hebrews 4:16 [NKJV]

9. 1 John 1:9 [NKJV]

10. Matthew 12:34 [NKJV]

11. Proverbs 4:23 [CSB]

12. Jeremiah 17:10 [NKJV]

13. Numbers 23:19 [ESV]

14. Genesis 1:26 [NKJV]

15. Matthew 5:16 [NKJV]

16. Ecclesiastes 5:5 [GNT]

17. Mark 12:31 [ESV]

18. Colossians 2:9 [NKJV]

19. Matthew 4:8-11 [ESV]

20. Daniel 1:4 [ESV]

21. Daniel 1:8 [ESV]

22. Daniel 6:3 [AMPC]

23. Daniel 6:4 [NKJV]

24. Number 13:27-28 [NKJV]

25. Revelations 12:10 [NKJV]

26. Romans 3:23 [ESV]

27. Romans 8:1 [CSB]

28. 2 Corinthians 5:21 [NKJV]

Chapter 5: The Love of an Excellent builder

1. 1 John 4:7 [NKJV]

2. John 13:34 [NKJV]

3. John 13:35 [NKJV]

4. 1 Corinthians 13:4-8 [CSB]

5. John 15:12-13 [ESV]

6. John 14:15 [NKJV]

7. Philippians 2:5 [MSG]

8. Philippians 2:8 [MSG]

9. Genesis 1:1 [NKJV]

10. Colossians 2:9 [NKJV]

11. Psalm 144:4 [TPT]

12. Psalm 121:1 [ESV]

13. Psalm 121:2 [ESV]

14. Isaiah 55:8 [NLT]

15. Isaiah 14:12-15 [NKJV]

16. Proverbs 19:20 [GNT]

Chapter 6: No Lone Wolves: With God, with people

1. Matthew 5:16 [AMP]

2. Psalm 119:105 [NKJV]

3. Luke 22:42 [CSB]

4. 1 Thessalonians 5:17 [NKJV ,GW, CSB]

5. Philippians 4:6 [NKJV]

6. Psalm 55:22 [ESV]

7. Psalm 37:7 [ESV]

8. Psalm 127:1 [NKJV]

9. John 6:63 [ESV]

10. 2 Timothy 3:16 [GNT]

11. John 4: 24 [NKJV]

12. Romans 12:2 [NKJV]

13. John 14:15 [ESV]

14. Luke 6:36 [ESV]

15. Galatians 6:2 [AMP]

16. Philippians 4:6-7 [TPT]

17. Ephesians 6:10 [ESV]

18. Proverbs 3:5 [NKJV]

19. Isaiah 1:19 [BSB]

20. Luke 11:15 [NLT]

21. Luke 11:28 [NLT]

22. Ecclesiastes 12:13 [NKJV]

23. Luke 5:16 [CSB]

24. Exodus 35:4-10 [NKJV]

25. Exodus 35:21 [NKJV]

26. Exodus 18:18 [NKJV]

27. Exodus 18:19-23 [NKJV]

Chapter 7: The Principled Builder

1. Ecclesiastes 3:4 [AMP]

2. Job 1:21 [AMP]

3. Daniel 3:17-18 [CSB]

4. 1 John 1:5 [TPT]

5. Deuteronomy 31:8 [NLT]

6. Romans 8:28 [NKJV]

7. Psalm 46:10 [AMPC]

8. Psalm 103:3 [NKJV]

9. Psalm 62:6 [GNT]

10. Joel 2:25 [ESV]

11. Matthew 7:9-11 [ESV]

12. John 15:14 [ESV]

13. Exodus 36:31-38 [AMP]

14. Philippians 1:6 [NKJV]

Chapter 8: The Excellent Steward

1. https://www.ncbi.nlm.nih.gov/pmc/articles/PMC4685725/#:~:t ext=Genes%20influence%20each%20individual%27s%20behavior al,and%20children%20within%20a%20family.

2. Psalm 127:3 [NLT]

3. Jeremiah 10:23 [NLT]

4. 1 Peter 4:10 [GW]

5. Genesis 1:26 [AMP]

6. Genesis 3:8 [NKJV]

7. 1 Corinthians 16:9 [AMP]

8. 1 Corinthians 4:1 [NLT]

9. 1 Corinth 4:2 [BSB]

10. 1 Peter 4:10 [GW]

11. Matthew 25:21 [NLT]

12. Philippians 4:12 [GNT]

13. Deuteronomy 8:18 [CSB]

14. Matthew 25:21 NLT

Chapter 9: The Idolatry of Excellence

1. Exodus 20:3-6 [NLT]

2. Psalm 29:2 [ESV]

3. Exodus 34:14 [NCV]

4. Philippians 2:13 [GNT]

5. Psalm 36:9 [GNT]

6. Philippians 4:19 [NKJV]

7. John 16:13 [AMP]

8. Genesis 11:3-4 [BSB]

9. 1 Corinthians 10:31 [ESV]

10. 1 Peter 4:10 [GW]

11. Genesis 11:8-9 [ESV]

12. Isaiah 55:11 [NKJV]

13. Jeremiah 29:11 [NKJV]

14. Psalm 1:3 [GNT]

15. Hebrews 4:16 [NKJV]

16. 1 John 1:9 [GNT]

17. Romans 3:23 [NLT]

18. Isaiah 41:10 [CSB]

Chapter 10: From My Community To You

1. Proverbs 10:21 [NLT]

About Author

Marthina is a certified life coach, with over a decade of experience in mentoring and coaching combined and a public speaker. Using the power of conversation through coaching, speaking engagements, writing and content creation, she specialises in nurturing and equipping individuals who find themselves amidst life's complex transitions. Her mission is to help others break free from chaos, embrace their true identity and confidently step into a future defined by clarity and purpose in excellence.

Her life call is rooted in Ephesians 4:12, to nurture and equip individuals so that they are able to fulfil the call of God on their life in an excellent manner, for the work of the ministry. It is her love for the Lord that fuels all that she does, and it's this call to nurture and equip individuals that all her work flows from. These include her YouTube channel, her coaching career, her speaking career, her masters in Christian Spirituality which explores the intersectionality between theology, psychology, history and culture and her current pursuit to obtain a certification in neuro-linguistic programming.

In 2021, she was featured in a Telegraph article where she shared her journey of transitioning from a student to a working adult and was recognised as one of UK's Top 100 Black Future leaders in 2020/2021 by the Future Leaders Magazine.

Connect with Marthina!

www.marthinaamarachi.com

info@marthinaamarachi.com

Marthina Amarachi on social platforms